Ugo Muccini

Palazzo Vecchio

Art Historical Guide
to the Palace
by Alessandro Cecchi

Scala

CONTENTS

Lay-out: Fulco Douglas Scotti
Translation: Lisa Pelletti
Photographs: Scala (M. Falsini, M. Sarri) except pp. 22, 23, 111, 112, 113, 114, 115, 125 (Fabbrica di Palazzo Vecchio)

Printed in Italy by Lito Terrazzi, Cascine del Riccio (Firenze),

Preface

The purpose of this book it to offer the visitor to Palazzo Vecchio a useful and practical guide, with general introductions to the palace and the square, ground-plans and illustrations, as well as a room by room art historical guide. We hope that this publication will help a greater number of people become acquainted with the palace, unfortunately quite frequently ignored by organized tourist itineraries through the city.
Palazzo Vecchio has always been a part of the history of Florence, for ever since earliest times it was the seat of the city's government.
To this day the palace still preserves a wealth of art treasures and the modern visitor can admire the changes and transformations that it has undergone over the years, dictated either by new practical needs or changing art fashions. Thus, we move from the original 14th-century nucleus, with its powerful tower and rusticated stone facing, to the sections of the palace that were restored in the Quattrocento, with their splendid carved ceilings decorated with gold, such as the Sala dell'Udienza and the Sala dei Gigli; through to the Apartments of the "Ducal Palace," which became the main part of the building after the modernizations commissioned by Cosimo I de' Medici, and carried out by the architect Tasso in the 1540s and 1550s, and by Giorgio Vasari after 1555.
Today's visitor will be able to admire those sections of the palace that have come down to us unaltered, and have been recently restored, like the Apartment of Leo X or the elegant Chapel of the Spanish-born Eleanor of Toledo; and he will be able to trace all the most important events of Florentine history from the Trecento down to the present in the rooms where they took place.
The artistic heritage of Palazzo Vecchio has recently acquired a new addition: one of the masterpieces of Quattrocento sculpture, Donatello's *Judith*, was removed from its position in the square, where it was exposed to all damages caused by the weather, and after being restored and cleaned by the Opificio delle Pietre Dure, is now on exhibit in the Sala dei Gigli.
The Palace was originally the residence of the Priors and the Gonfalonier of Justice, who lived here permanently, alternating every two months; later it became the residence of Duke Cosimo and his Court, until the first nucleus of the new Pitti Palace was built in the second half of the 16th century. It was given the name "Vecchio" when the Medici Court was transferred to the new palace on the other side of the Arno, to which it was connected via the Uffizi Gallery and the Vasari Corridor. But Palazzo Vecchio has always been the seat of the government and magistracies of Florence, even at the time of the Lorraine dynasty and after the Unification of Italy; at present, it houses the Mayor's office and all the offices of the local government administration as well as the Town Council meetings.

View from Via de' Cerchi

PIAZZA DELLA SIGNORIA

by Ugo Muccini

The construction of the square, historically connected to the Palazzo dei Priori, was tied to the developments of the palace, for it was always conceived as the space where the meetings of the people's "parliaments" were held or the official public ceremonies of the city of Florence, and it had to be suitably large and grand.
Florence was a medieval city, with narrow streets, and tower-houses built up against each other: there were no open spaces at all. When the houses belonging to the Ghibelline family Uberti were torn down, the city magistrates chose that area as the site for the new palace that was to house the Priors and the Gonfalonier of Justice. This was in December 1298 and the magistrates also deliberated to buy the houses nearby, some to be demolished, others to be incorporated into the new construction. The site was chosen also because it was fairly close to the Palace of the Captain of the People, later the Palace of the Podestà (today it houses the Bargello National Museum) and to the church of San Piero Scheraggio (today incorporated into the building of the Uffizi), which until 1313 was where the supreme Council of the city's government met.
In an age of violent internecine strife between the city's various factions and social classes, it was also necessary to provide a wide expanse of open ground around the palace, so as to make its defence easier. To this day the palace still looks like a stronghold or a fortress.
Starting in the beginning of the 14th century we have records of allocations for the widening of the square and for its paving which was commissioned in 1319: a brickwork paving with a geometric grid in pietra serena flagstones.
The Priors of the city had been granted absolute freedom of action in their plans for enlarging the square "pro decore et fortificatione palatii populi Florentini" (for the glory and the fortification of the palace of the Florentine people). But they did come up against certain unsurmountable architectural barriers, such as the churches of San Romolo and Santa Cecilia and the houses and shops alongside the magistrates' new palace. When Walter de Brienne, Duke of Athens, came to power in 1342, he decided to go ahead with the idea of tearing down these buildings, for he wanted to turn the Palazzo dei Priori into an impregnable castle. The Church was naturally opposed to the project and his rule was too short-lived—he was deposed by a popular insurrection in 1343—to allow him to carry it out. Finally, in the second half of the century, a solution was found: the churches, houses and shops were torn down and rebuilt a bit further away from the palace. The church of San Romolo was demolished in 1356 and rebuilt right away, as were the nearby houses, finished by 1362.
In 1364 the Portico of the Pisans was built on the spot where today the building of Assicurazioni Generali stands; its name comes from the fact that it was built by Pisan prisoners after Florence's victory over Pisa.
Then, between 1374 and 1382, the Loggia was built under the supervision of Benci di Cione and Francesco Talenti and decorated with statues of the Virtues made between 1384 and 1389 by Jacopo di Piero Guidi and Giovanni d'Ambrogio. The Loggia, today known as Loggia dell'Orcagna (who probably designed the construction) or Loggia dei Lanzi (because it was here that the Lanzichenecchi guards had their encampment at the time of Cosimo I in the 16th century), was originally intended as the dais for the members of the Seigneury during public ceremonies. Next to it was the Aringhiera, a sort of raised platform that surrounded the palace, where the Priors and the Gonfalonier of Justice presided over solemn celebrations; the Aringhiera was demolished in 1812, at the time of the French occupation.

Around 1385 the brick paving of the square was begun; the operation was supervised by the Opera di Santa Maria del Fiore. It was at this time that the church of Santa Cecilia, near Via Vacchereccia, was torn down. Shortly after 1359, the Palazzo della Mercatanzia had been built on the northeastern side of the square: it is still there today and still preserves the emblems of the Guilds on its facade. Since 1345 the Executor of the Ordnances of Justice

◁
Giovanni Stradano
Piazza della Signoria on the Feastday of St John the Baptist, the Patron Saint of Florence (Palazzo Vecchio)

Piazza della Signoria

and Conduct Officer had their headquarters in Via dei Gondi.
In the second half of the Trecento the statue of the *Marzocco* lion was placed at one end of the Aringhiera, where Ammannati's fountain is today. The Marzocco lion was the symbol of the city of Florence and a number of live lions were kept in cages at first in front of the church of San Piero Scheraggio and later behind the palace, on the street called Via dei Leoni.
In the Quattrocento the square continued to serve the same function it had had in the previous century: all official ceremonies were held here, most religious processions culminated here and all the city's festive celebrations were organized in it. In 1495, after the Medici had been expelled from Florence and the city was proclaimed a Republic, one of Donatello's masterpieces, Judith and Holofernes, was moved here from the garden of the Medici Palace in Via Larga: it was placed on the Aringhiera as a symbol of civic and republican virtues.
The bronze sculpture of David, also by Donatello, was placed inside the palace, in the entrance courtyard; it had also been in the garden of the Medici Palace (today it is in the Bargello).
On 23 May 1498 the Dominican preacher Fra Girolamo Savonarola and two of his followers were hanged and burnt at the stake in the square. Savonarola had advocated the new republican government and had fostered the deep religious and social reforms that had taken place in the city in those last years of the century. A round marble inscription recalls to this day the exact spot where the execution took place: the Dominican friars from the monastery of San Marco, where Savonarola had taken his vows, still pay homage to him on this spot.
In 1504 a group of important artists and citizens deliberated to transfer the statue of

The Loggia dei Lanzi

The Fountain in Piazza della Signoria, called the "Biancone" (by Bartolomeo Ammannati and assistants)

David by Michelangelo from the yard of the Opera del Duomo, where the artist had been working on it, to the square; it was placed on the Aringhiera instead of Donatello's *Judith* to the left of the main entrance to the palace. Today the original sculpture is in the Academy; what we see in the square is a copy made in 1873.
Donatello's *Judith* was moved inside the Palazzo Vecchio, but two years later was transferred outside again, under the righthand arch of the Loggia, the one nearest Via Vacchereccia; it stayed there until 1583 when it was replaced by Giambologna's *Rape of the Sabine Women*.
At the time of the tyrannical rule of Duke Alessandro de' Medici, Baccio Bandinelli sculpted his group of *Hercules and Cacus*, which was placed on the corner of the square leading to Via della Ninna on 1 May 1534. Dating from just a few years later, during the reign of Cosimo I, are the two marble statues on either side of the main door of the palace; they are the work of Baccio Bandinelli and his collaborator Vincenzo de' Rossi.
In the early years of the reign of Cosimo I de' Medici, the newly nominated Duke of Florence, Benvenuto Cellini, Court sculptor, cast his *Perseus* (1545-54); it was placed under the first arch (nearest the palace) of the Loggia, where it still is today. In 1559 Giorgio Vasari completed his final project for the construction of the Uffizi, the central headquarters of the administration of the Medici State. Work on the building began that same year. In 1580 the building was finished and it extended from the Loggia in the square all the way to the river. The new Grand Duke Francesco I transformed the top floor of the building into a gallery containing all the family's art collections and created craft workshops of various kinds.
In 1563 work was begun on the fountain in the middle of the square; the project was drawn up-

Giambologna
The Rape of the Sabine Women

Benvenuto Cellini
Perseus

by Bartolomeo Ammannati and work continued until 1575, demolishing part of the 14th-century Aringhiera in the process. At the centre of the fountain is the large marble statue of *Neptune*, familiarly called *Biancone* (huge white one) by the Florentines, surrounded by bronze statues of *Tritons* and *Nereids*, some of which are the work of the Flemish-born sculptor Giambologna. The fountain is one of the masterpieces of Mannerist sculpture and is also one of the most successful pieces of urban decoration designed at the time of Cosimo I.

The sculptor of Flemish origin, Giambologna,

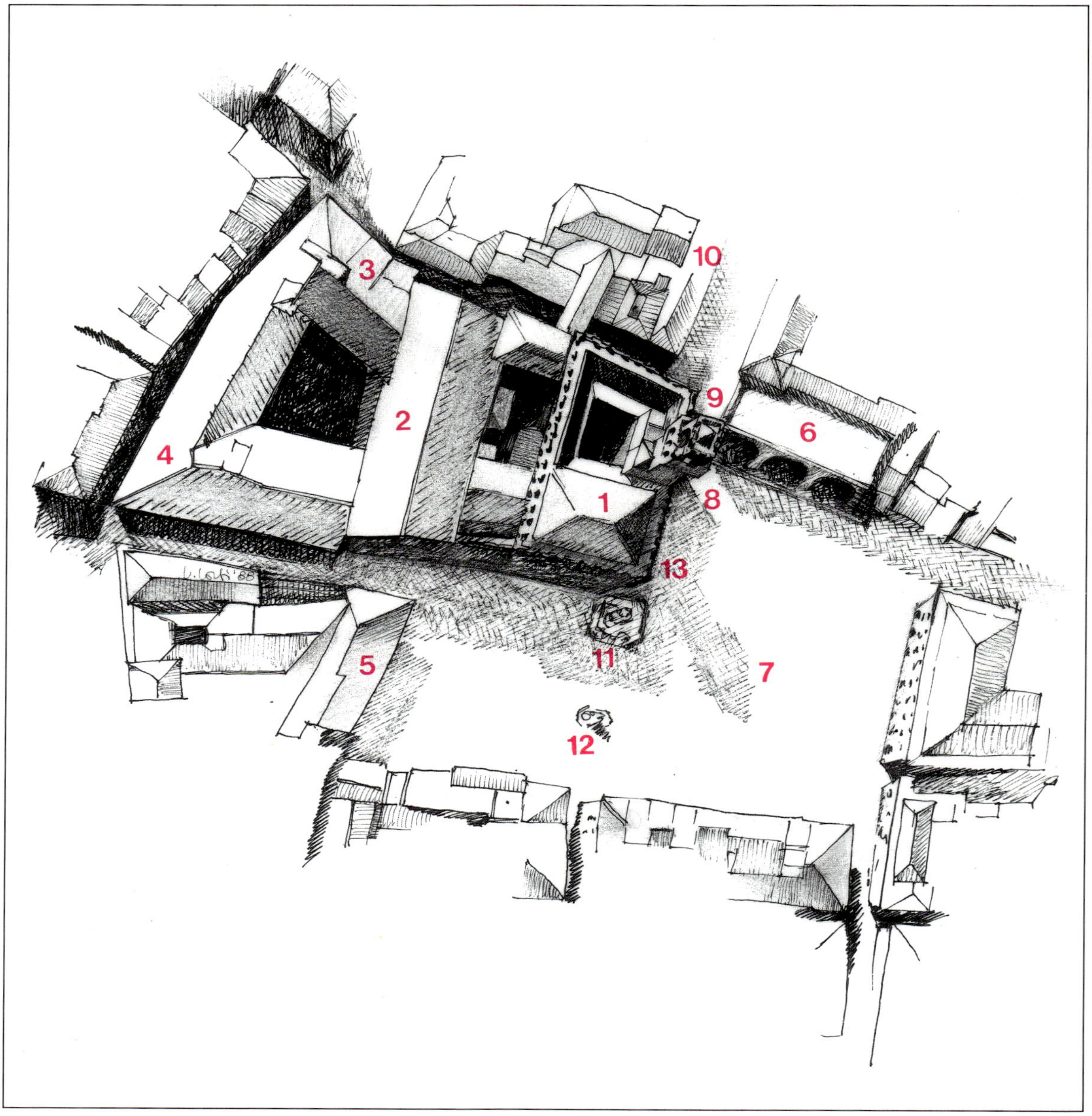

Palazzo Vecchio and Piazza della Signoria

1. The 14th-century nucleus of the palace
2. Salone dei Cinquecento
3. Enlargement designed by Battista del Tasso
4. Addition built at the time of Ferdinand I
5. Palazzo della Mercatanzia
6. Loggia dei Lanzi
7. Plaque commemorating the execution of Savonarola
8. Copy of Michelangelo's *David*
9. *Hercules and Cacus*
10. The Uffizi
11. Fountain of Neptune, called the "Biancone"
12. Equestrian statue of Cosimo I
13. Copy of Donatello's *Judith*

Giambologna
Equestrian statue of Cosimo I de' Medici

after his collaboration on the fountain, became Francesco I's and Ferdinand I's Court artist. The last important sculptures to be placed in the square in the late Cinquecento were his, in particular the extremely famous and popular *Rape of the Sabine Women* (1583) which anticipates the spatial and formal research of the following century; it replaced Donatello's *Judith* under the righthand arch of the Loggia. His next statue was the equestrian monument to *Cosimo I*, commissioned by Ferdinand I to honour his father's memory in 1587; it was not completed until 1594. The last sculpture by Giambologna to be placed in the square was the *Hercules and Nessus*, finished in 1599 and put under the Loggia dei Lanzi.
In the 18th century, at the time of the Lorraine family rule, the two lions guarding the entrance to the Loggia were installed: the righthand one is a classical sculpture, whereas the other is a copy by the Roman artist Flaminio Vacca (16th century). They were brought here from the Loggia of the Medici Villa in Rome, as were the other classical statues now in the Loggia, like the *Menelaus* (or perhaps it is Ajax) *Holding the Body of Patroclus* and the six Roman empresses or matrons lined up against the end wall. In 1866 Pio Fedi carved his marble group of the *Rape of Polyxena*, which was also put under the Loggia, by this stage a real open-air museum and no longer the place where the public ceremonies of the city of Florence were held.
In 1812, when the Aringhiera was definitively

demolished by architect Giuseppe Del Rosso, the pietra serena *Marzocco* sculpted in 1418-20 for the Pope's apartments in Santa Maria Novella by Donatello was set up on the 15th-century carved plinth, decorated with the coats-of-arms of the Republic of Florence, where the original *Marzocco* had stood. But in 1885 Donatello's sculpture was removed to the Bargello National Museum and replaced by a copy, which can still be admired today on the steps leading up to the palace, near Ammannati's fountain.

PALAZZO VECCHIO THROUGH THE CENTURIES

by Ugo Muccini

Construction of Palazzo Vecchio was begun in 1299. It was planned as a headquarters for the city's magistrature, and was commissioned by the Council of the Hundred on a proposal advanced by Giano della Bella, the author of the "Ordnances of Justice" passed in 1293, which excluded the Florentine aristocracy from holding public offices. But in order to understand the historical and political significance of the palace better, we must take a step further back. In the 13th century Florence witnessed the struggle between Guelphs and Ghibellines, the two factions that fought for supremacy over the city. But neither realized that an alternative power was rising, that is the class of merchants and bankers, which was beginning to organize its activities with the creation of Corporations and Guilds; the members of this class were fully aware of their potentialities and the fact that they were now in a position to take over from the feudal aristocracy, worn out by their internecine struggles. The Ghibellines remained in power only until 1250, the year the Swabian King Frederick II died. After this the bourgeois Guelphs succeeded in overthrowing the aristocratic Ghibellines and formed the government that was known as the "Primo Popolo." Just ten years after that, the Ghibellines managed to return to power in the city; but in 1266 the defeat of Manfred of

Unknown 15th-century artist
Map of the Catena, detail of Palazzo Vecchio

Swabia at the battle of Benevento marked the definitive loss of power of both the Swabians and the Ghibellines.
At this point the Guelph faction, made up of the wealthy merchants and bankers as well as a section of the aristocracy which had not taken part in earlier struggles, took over the government of Florence, entirely excluding the poorer classes, such as the artisans and small-scale traders who had in the meantime organized themselves into the Minor Guilds. This exclusion from power of the rising economic categories produced internal contrasts and clashes, and eventually the "constitution" had to be amended, attributing greater power to the Priors of the Guilds, who represented the Minor Guilds as well. In the 1293 Ordnances of Justice the number of Guilds was increased and the office of Gonfalonier of Justice was created; the Gonfalonier was a supreme magistrate representing the people and his authority was enforced by a militia of armed soldiers. The Commune was administered by the Priors and the Gonfalonier jointly. "Thus the Guilds had taken hold of the State which had become a people's government, the likes of which had no equal in history," as Gino Capponi concludes in his *History of the Florentine Republic* (1875).
The need to build a new palace was expressed already in 1285 when, in a meeting held in the church of Santa Reparata, it was decided that a suitable location be found; but it was only later, in July 1294, that the site was chosen and the first contacts with the owners of the houses and land that had to be expropriated were made. The area chosen was between the church of San Piero Scheraggio and the ruins of the houses of the Uberti family, members of the Ghibelline faction. Giovanni Villani, writing in the 14th century, explains why this area was chosen "and in order for the palace not to be on the land of the Uberti, those responsible for drawing up the plans laid it out at an angle, so that it was difficult to build it square and further away from the church of San Piero Scheraggio (. . .) and where they laid the foundations of the palace there had previously stood the houses of the rebel Uberti family, Florentine Ghibellines, and those houses were razed to the ground. . ."
The construction site of the new palace became a focal point in the urban structure of the city, fitting into the Sestiere of San Piero Scheraggio, on the edge of the original Roman city. The foundations for the new building were begun on 24 February 1299; at the same time it was decided to buy a further group of houses which would then be pulled down so as to widen the square. The design of the palace and its tower is attributed to Arnolfo di Cambio, but even Villani in his "Chronicle" never mentions the name of any architect when he writes of the construction. It was only much later that Vasari stated that Arnolfo had given the building "an appearance similar to that of the palace his own father had built in the Casentino for the Counts of Poppi."
Construction probably began from the side facing San Piero Scheraggio, around some existing houses into which the Priors and the Gonfalonier had moved since the beginning of 1299. One of the first things to be built was the wing that joins onto the Foraboschi tower which, like all the other towers in the city, had had its top lopped off in 1250 (they had all been reduced to a maximum height of 50 *braccia*, about 29 metres). At first the tower was probably used as it was; some time before 1301 the bell from the previous residence of the city's Priors, the houses of the Cerchi family near the church of San Procolo, was placed in it.
Already on 26 March 1302 an important meeting, in the presence of the Priors and the Gonfalonier, was held in the palace; but it was not until 24 March 1313 that the supreme Councils of the Commune were definitively transferred to the Council Hall built especially for them in the northern wing of the Priors' Palace.
In the meantime the courtyard had been built, the tower had been raised, and the Sala d'Arme on the ground floor had been completed. (The great hall of the Sala d'Arme is the only one that still preserves its original medieval appearance to this day.) In 1315 building work on the palace was virtually completed.
At the time the palace was begun the city was once again divided into two factions, the White Guelphs and the Black Guelphs. The Whites were in favour of a policy of independence and sympathized with the Emperor, like the Ghibellines before them, while the Blacks supported the Papacy and the French. The Blacks soon imposed their supremacy and exiled the Whites (Dante Alighieri was among the Whites who were thrown out of the city), but the Florentine Republic was finding it increasingly difficult to maintain its hegemony over the other cities of Tuscany, and eventual-

Palazzo Vecchio and its relationship to the rest of the city

ly had to ask for help from the Pope and the French. In 1309 the Anjou dynasty was conferred the title of "honorary Seigneurs" of the city, with the complicity of the lower merchant classes and against the wishes of the bourgeoisie. This government, which was nominated yearly, lasted until 1342, when the Duke of Athens, Walter de Brienne, was made Seigneur for life by Robert of Anjou.

That was also the year in which the first radical alterations of the palace took place, for construction was by that stage over. The Duke, the usurper of the free government of the Commune, started by imposing his rule over the Florentines by force. The first measure he took was to have the palace fortified, ordering that huge walls be built in front of the main doorway and the entrance to the Sala d'Arme; he fortified the wing where the Salone dei Cinquecento now is and he extended the palace's defence structures as far as what is now the corner between Via della Ninna and Via dei Leoni. As a further measure of defence, the Duke had also planned to widen the square, tearing down the remaining houses and the nearby churches of San Piero Scheraggio, Santa Cecilia and San Romolo. All these fortifications were planned and carried out, at least according to Vasari, by Andrea Pisano, but there are no documents to prove this theory. The

rule of the Duke of Athens did not last long, only until 26 July 1343, the feastday of St Anne, when a popular uprising besieged the palace and forced the Duke to flee from the city. There is a painting that depicts this event, a fresco that was found in the ancient prisons of the Stinche; it has been detached and now hangs in the "Salotta" on the second floor of the palace.
This fresco is an important document for it shows the appearance of the Palazzo Vecchio after all the fortifications that the Duke of Athens had commissioned. We can clearly distinguish the two fortified openings protecting the doorway of the Sala d'Arme and the main entrance: they are as tall as the first floor windows and are joined to a defence wall that conceals also the "Aringhiera" (or debate balcony) that the Seigneury had had built towards the end of 1323. At the time of this painting the tower was practically finished, for it lacked only the cusp: this was not actually installed till August 1453, together with the gilded copper pennant in the shape of a lion rampant topped by a trefoiled fleur-de-lys. The outside of the palace was built rather like a fortress, as it still is today; its walls are in rusticated stone with pietra serena divisions between the different stories; the ground floor windows are very high and protected by iron bars, while the windows of the upper floors are two-light mullioned windows displaying both the Florentine fleur-de-lys and the people's cross.
Above the main doorway we find the coat-of-arms of Christ the King, an emblem that is very Republican in feeling and was not placed here until 1528; it stands between two gilded lions against a blue background with gold fleur-de-lys (which were already there) and alongside the inscription "Iesus Christus, Rex Florentini Populi S.P. Decreto electus" (Jesus Christ, King of the Florentine People, elected by Decree of the People's Senate). This was replaced in 1851 by the inscription we see today: "Rex regum at Dominus dominatium" (King of Kings and Lord of Lordships).
The smaller windows on the righthand side of the tower are those of the mezzanine between the first and second floors, whereas the square ones on the lefthand side and on the side facing Via dei Gondi serve only as air vents for the wooden structure of the ceiling of the Council Hall (now Sala dei Dugento) and the loft above the present Sala dell'Udienza and Sala dei Gigli. The gallery around the building, which projects slightly from the facade and is supported by stone corbels ("beccatelli") joined to one another by round arches, is the part of the palace specifically designed to guarantee its defence. The gallery contains two walkways: the lower one is covered and has look-outs, arrow-slits and trap-doors built into the floor above the doors and windows of the facade. Above this covered walkway there is another one, without a roof but protected by huge square crenellations. The gallery runs all the way around the medieval palace and is decorated with painted coats-of-arms of the Republic of Florence; starting from the lefthand side they are the emblems of the Captain of the People (red cross on a white field), of the Guelph city (red fleur-de-lys on a white field), of Florence and of Fiesole (white and red shield, the colours of the Republic), of the Papacy (two crossed keys on a blue field), of the Seigneury (the motto LIBERTAS in gold letters on a blue field), of the Guelph faction (a red eagle on a green dragon and a gold fleur-de-lys on its head), of the Ghibelline city (white fleur-de-lys on a red field), of Charles and Robert of Anjou (gold fleur-de-lys on a blue field with a red label), of Louis of Anjou, King of Hungary (divided shield with gold fleur-de-lys on a blue field to the right and white and red bands to the left).
During the course of the 14th century the new building witnessed the conflicts between the populace and the rich mercantile bourgeoisie, culminating in a bloody uprising, the riot of the Ciompi in 1378, brutally repressed by a government which was becoming increasingly authoritarian, gradually abolishing all the civilized institutions of the Commune and the Republic. In 1434, when Cosimo de' Medici returned from exile, despite the appearances of a Republican government, all effective power became concentrated in his hands for he was entirely responsible for the nominations to the major offices, all of which he carefully placed in the hands of his loyal supporters.
In 1446 a new office was created, the Palace "Operai," whose task it was to supervise all restorations and renovations of the Palazzo della Signoria, as it was now called.
The Medici family, in particular Cosimo the Elder, realized that the palace needed to be transformed, to be made more comfortable for the Priors and the Gonfalonier who lived there; and so the complex restructurations began. The renovations continued in the following century as well, when work was commissioned and supervised by Cosimo I, Duke of Tuscany, who turned the palace into his own residence and court. The transformations were

Detail of the main doorway, with the frieze and the two "termini"

begun by Michelozzo di Bartolomeo, a friend of Cosimo the Elder and his favourite architect. In 1454 work started on the courtyard, where it appears that a whole series of "rooms and little rooms" as contemporary chroniclers put it, had rather hastily been built up against the defence walls without following a real project. Michelozzo's idea was to widen the courtyard, to make it more spacious, to add new windows; he also built a portico to make the entrance to the palace more attractive. The walls of the courtyard were divided into *graffito* panels, with gold fleur-de-lys on a grey background, a decoration that has today disappeared except for some small patches that were rediscovered during the recent restorations.
As well as on the courtyard, Michelozzo worked on the main stairway and on other parts of the palace: he built the mezzanine and reinforced the tower. Even Brunelleschi, as we learn from his biographer Antonio Manetti, worked in the palace just before 1446, the year he died; but unfortunately there is no trace today of anything he may have designed.
The sculptor and architect Benedetto da Maiano worked in the palace some time around 1472, dividing the huge room above the Council Hall into two smaller ones, the Sala dell'Udienza and the Sala dei Gigli. The dividing wall he built involved a rather complex carpentry operation with two huge wooden beams being placed under the floor and the construction of an enormous round arch; the partition walls, two brick structures with a 30 cm interspace between them, were suspended from the arch by iron tie-beams. The most extraordinary aspect of this project were the splendid ceilings, carved, painted and gilded, and the graceful marble frame around the doorway joining the two rooms: the wooden doors are the work of Benedetto's brother Giuliano and of Francione.
When the Medici were expelled from the city in 1494 and Florence was declared a Republic, the palace became the headquarters of a government that was no longer in the hands of councils formed by small numbers of representatives, but one which was founded on the consultation of ever larger sections of the population. The construction of a new and much larger Council Hall became necessary, for the existing one, the one that today is known as Sala dei Dugento, was not big enough.
One of the most active supporters of this political reform was Fra Girolamo Savonarola who had often incited the Florentines to give themselves a "popular government like the one they have in Venice," as a contemporary defined it. The new Council Hall was in fact designed on the model of the huge room in the Doges' Palace where the Grand Council met.
The idea of building a new room for the Council meetings is normally attributed to Fra Girolamo Savonarola, but actually the need to build a new Hall had been expressed as early as 1452. The old Council Hall was no longer large enough to contain the meetings of the citizenry, for the size of the population was constantly growing, both because of natural demographic increase and because of the arrival of many families of exiles from Naples and Venice. The project was not carried out at that time for lack of funds.
On 12 December 1494 Savonarola said: "I believe that the Government the Venetians have is very good; we should not be ashamed to learn from others, for they were given their Government by God, and since they have had it, there has never been any form of civic dissent among them." And following the model of Venice the friar proposed that a new Council be formed, consisting of a thousand citizens of proven honesty. The new constitution was approved on 23 December 1494 and the old Parliament, which in the hands of the Medici had become simply an instrument to perpetuate their autocracy, was dissolved. In order to meet, this new Council needed a huge meeting room and it was resolved that the new construction should be built at the back of the palace, overlooking the Captain's Courtyard, the Customs office and the other buildings dating from the time of the Duke of Athens. The commission was given to Simone del Pollaiolo, known as Cronaca, on 15 July 1495.
Construction work on the new room began shortly thereafter and in February 1496 Landucci recorded that "the Seigneury retired to the New Room which had a roof over it but had no floor tiles and no benches. The door joining the Palace to the Hall was finished; everything else was begun, but nothing was complete." Work had progressed so rapidly that in just over nine months the new hall could already be used for a council meeting, and only a few months later, in May that year, we learn that "the brick tiling of the Great Council Hall was finished." Two years later, in November 1498, the woodcarver Clemente del Tasso finished the central part of the ceiling, depicting the coat-of-arms of the People surrounded by the eight emblems of Florence, the Commune, the Guelph faction and the Patron Saints. The last details were completed much

The facade on Via dei Leoni

more slowly and work was not finished until 1502. The Great Council Hall, later called the Sala dei Cinquecento or Hall of the Five Hundred, also contained the seats for the magistrates, surrounded by banisters and with steps leading up to them; the Council members sat in row chairs divided by aisles by which one could reach the main entrance to the room. At the end of the Hall there was the dais for the Seigneury and the Chapel with a pulpit.

The Ricetto, the little room connecting the old Council Hall (the Sala dei Dugento) and the new Hall, was finished in 1505.

The new Hall was built 38 *braccia* behind the back wall of the original building; its shape follows the slanting line of the streets that surround it, Via dei Gondi to the north and Via della Ninna to the south. In his description of the Council Hall Vasari gives the following measurements: 38 *braccia* (22.19 metres) deep, length of the west wall 90 *braccia* (52.56 metres), of the east wall 106 *braccia* (61.90 metres), and a height of 20 *braccia* (11.68 metres). He also describes the Hall before the alterations he himself designed in 1563 for Duke Cosimo, including the raising of the ceiling by about 12 *braccia* (7 metres): "The two end walls of this room were not at right angles: at each side they were eight *braccia* out of plumb. So, they did not, as they might have done, decide to increase the thickness of the walls to remedy this; they raised the height of the walls as they stood and put in three windows on each one of the end walls. But once they had finished, the room was so large that it did not have sufficient lighting, and it was also not tall enough considering its length and its width, so that it appeared dwarfed and altogether disproportionate. They tried to improve on it, but without much success, by opening two windows in the centre of the east wall and four in the west wall."

From this description and other similar ones by contemporaries we can reconstruct which wall Michelangelo and Leonardo found enough space on to paint their huge battle scenes, commissioned by Gonfalonier Pier Soderini. It was the east wall that only had two windows, and the Seigneury's dais in between them. Leonardo and Michelangelo were called upon some time in 1503 or 1504 to decorate the room with two frescoes: they each made a cartoon depicting a battle won by the Florentine Republic in the 14th and 15th centuries. Leonardo drew the battle of Anghiari (1440) and Michelangelo the battle of Cascina, in the war against Pisa (1364). But only Leonardo actually began to transpose the cartoon onto the wall, and he did this with an experimental technique, similar to the methods used by the ancient Romans in their encaustic painting. Vasari describes it like this: "Since he wanted to paint on the wall in oils, he made a very oily

Detail of the eaves designed by Tasso

and thick mixture for laying on the wall; but, as he continued to paint in the same room, it began to run in such a way that he soon abandoned the idea, for he saw that it was ruined."

From Vasari's words we learn that Leonardo abandoned the project, and Michelangelo did the same. For a long time the cartoons remained in the palace, where they were much admired and studied by other artists; unfortunately, they were handled so much that they were eventually ruined.

When the Medici returned to Florence in 1512 the Hall was actually turned into a barracks for the soldiers. The family that had ruled the city in the previous century decided, however, to establish their residence in the original family palace in Via Larga, Palazzo Medici. This period was followed by the brief Republican interlude (1527-30) and the short-lived reign of Duke Alessandro de' Medici, assassinated in 1537 by Lorenzino de' Medici.

In 1540 Cosimo de' Medici, who had been elected Duke of Florence a few years earlier by imperial decree, moved his family and the court from the Medici family palace to Palazzo della Signoria. This marked the beginning of the transformations that the palace underwent in order to satisfy the new needs of the court; in a short time the palace was changed from the austere seat of the Priors and the Gonfalonier of Justice that it had been into a splendid Ducal Palace. Among the many parts of the palace that were radically transformed, the first to be altered was the huge Council Hall: there was no longer any need for a large space for popular assemblies and Cosimo I decided that he would give a first demonstration of his absolute political power by having it turned into a grandiose reception room.

The first architects to be called upon were Giuliano di Baccio d'Agnolo and Baccio Bandinelli who were commissioned the construction of the "Udienza." This is conceived rather like a stage in the centre of which the ducal throne was placed; it rests on a dais with four steps leading up to it. The architectural design, with its classical style columns, monumental windows and niches containing statues of famous members of the Medici family, is rather reminiscent of a grandiose Roman triumphal arch. The statues in the niches and the lavish ornamentation are the work of several other artists as well; the project was not completed until 1594.

For the south side of the room, opposite the Udienza, around 1555 Bartolomeo Ammannati was commissioned a fountain, but it was never completed (the statues which were supposed to decorate it are today in the courtyard of the Bargello Museum). This fountain was intended to cancel forever any memories of the original function of the Hall during Republican times. It was around this same period (1554-55) that the woodcarver Giovan Battista di Marco del Tasso worked in the palace as an architect. He was responsible for the project for the new stairway from the Sala dei Cinquecento, through the Sala dei Gigli, up to the second floor. This stairway, a fairly elegant construction with two landings, was built where Cronaca's stairway ended originally (that is, where the Studiolo now is) and it was placed against the wall parallel to the back wall of the old palace; it led to a loggia and a large room that was used as an antechamber (today it is the Room of Maps) and through which one entered the Sala dei Gigli, or perhaps the room above the Ricetto, today called the Chancery. Tasso was officially the "architect of the Palace walls" and in this capacity he built new rooms and stairways in the wing overlooking Via della Ninna, enlarging the building all the way to Via dei Leoni. Under his supervision several rooms were redesigned and he had some terraces built, like the Duchess's terrace, with decorations by Bachiacca, which was constructed between the original 14th-century structure and the Salone dei Cinquecento on the south side. He also designed the Apartment of the Elements and the huge rusticated stone doorway surmounted by the Duke's coat-of-arms in Via dei Leoni.

At around the same time that architect Giovan Battista del Tasso was altering and transforming the austere Republican palace into a comfortable residence for Duke Cosimo, two Flemish masters were called to Florence: Jan Rost (died 1564) and Nicholaus Karcher (died 1562) set up the Medici tapestry factory and produced twenty tapestries depicting stories from the life of Joseph from the Old Testament, woven on cartoons by Bronzino (1503-1572), Pontormo (1494-1557) and Salviati (1510-1563). These tapestries normally hung in the Sala dei Dugento, but only ten at a time and on important occasions. (In the 18th century and the first half of the 19th these tapes-

The corner on Via della Ninna

The tower

tries were kept in the Guardaroba; in 1865 the series was divided into two sections, one for Palazzo Vecchio and the other for Palazzo Pitti. Since 1872 half of the tapestries have hung uninterruptedly in the Sala dei Dugento, whereas the other half were transferred to Rome in 1887 to decorate the rooms of the Quirinal Palace. The tapestries hanging on the walls of the Sala dei Dugento were removed in 1983 and the first restoration analyses were carried out; in 1986 a restoration laboratory was set up in Palazzo Vecchio itself, in the Room of the Flags, and the restoration of the precious tapestries is now well underway.)

When Tasso died on 8 May 1555 he was replaced by Giorgio Vasari, who had already been in the Duke's employ since January of that year. For the next nineteen years, until the death of both the Duke and the artist in 1574 that is, not a brick in the palace was moved without the approval of the artist from Arezzo.

In particular Vasari devoted a great deal of attention to the construction of new staircases, wider and more comfortable, more suited to a princely residence. All the medieval stairways were torn down or redesigned; Cronaca's stairway, a single flight that led up to the Salone dei Cinquecento, was demolished, as were Tasso's and the one that led up to the second floor. The new one that was built in the area between the 14th-century construction and the Salone dei Cinquecento starts from the space between Michelozzo's courtyard and the courtyard of the Dogana, or Customs; it is a double ramp stairway and reaches both the Sala dei Dugento and the Salone dei Cinquecento through the Ricetto. From the Ricetto another stairway, smaller but not so steep (the "flat" stairway, as it is called), leads to the mezzanine and the second floor, where it joins the 14th-century stairway that goes from the anteroom between the Salotta and the Sala dei Gigli up to the kitchen area and the tower.

Vasari began to work on the new stairway in 1560 and finished it around the middle of 1564. The new construction involved the demolition or transformation of many sections of the palace, to the extent that today we are not able to reconstruct exactly what it was like before his intervention. In the course of these restructuring operations Vasari created new rooms, mostly very small ones, hollowed out from the walls of the earlier building; these became studies and sitting rooms for the Duke's personal use. On the side overlooking Via della Ninna he created a writing room, which later became the Studiolo of Francesco I, Cosimo's son, and the "Tesoretto," a small study used by Cosimo. The Duke's bathroom was installed below the first flight of the stairway. Giorgio Vasari worked in the Palazzo Vecchio from 1555 till his death and totally transformed the appearance of the palace. In 1555 he began by redesigning the Apartments of Leo X (on the first floor, next to the Salone dei Cinquecento), in collaboration with Cosimo Bartoli (1503-1572). Construction work on this apartment continued until 1562 and the rooms, recently restored, were dedicated to illustrious members of the Medici family: they were used as official reception rooms. Above the Apartments of Leo X, on the second floor, Vasari created the Apartment of the Elements; he worked here, assisted by several talented collaborators, from 1555 to 1558, and following another iconographical programme drawn up by the learned Cosimo Bartoli, dedicated the decoration of the rooms to the gods of classical mythology. This iconographical programme was seen as a companion piece to the decoration of the Apartments of Leo X on the floor below, where Vasari had celebrated the "earthly" gods, the Medici dynasty.

Between 1561 and 1562 Vasari worked on a group of rooms that had been the residence of the Priors at the time of the Republic; they were on the second floor of the medieval part of the building. He completed the Apartments of Eleanor of Toledo, the wife of Duke Cosimo, which had already been begun in the 1540s by Tasso who had designed the Green Room (with frescoes by Ridolfo del Ghirlandaio), the Chapel (with frescoes by Bronzino) and the small study with decorations by Salviati. These rooms illustrate the stories of famous women from antiquity, but the Duchess never lived here, for she died of malaria in Pisa in 1562.

Between 1562 and 1565 Vasari raised the ceiling and redesigned the Salone dei Cinquecento, rearranging the Room of Maps by transforming a loggia that was used as a landing for Tasso's stairway. In just a few months in 1565 Vasari also built the corridor that connects Palazzo Vecchio to Palazzo Pitti through the Uffizi Gallery, over Ponte Vecchio. That same year the Duke also asked Vasari to supervise the preparations in the palace and throughout the city for his son Francesco's wedding to Princess Joan of Austria. Cosimo gave Vasari an unlimited budget for these wedding preparations and the architect gave his imagination free rein. Im Palazzo Vecchio, among other in-

The doorway on Via dei Leoni

novations, the courtyard that had already been redesigned in the 15th century by Michelozzo was completely transformed: the columns were covered with plant motif decorations in gilded stuccowork, with putti and other figures, while the ceilings of the portico were decorated with grotesques and the walls were covered with views of the major cities of "Austria, Bohemia, Hungary and the Tyrol" in honour of the Hapsburgs. In 1570, the crown prince Francesco de' Medici commissioned Vasari to decorate his study, which he wanted to transform into a chamber containing his collections of rare and precious objects. The elaborate decoration programme was drawn up by Vincenzo Borghini and the small room, today called the Studiolo, was created out of the hollow spaces in the thick palace walls near the Tesoretto; it was in direct communication with the prince's rooms and also with a narrow stairway that leads out onto the street, on Via della Ninna. The transformation of the Studiolo was probably the last project that Vasari embarked upon before he died on 27 June 1574. Two months earlier, on 21 April, his great patron Cosimo I, the founder of the Medici State and the man who had commissioned all these exceptional reconstruction projects in the palace, had died. In 1569 the Medicis had become Grand Dukes. Cosimo was succeeded by his son Francesco, under whose rule no further work was carried out on the palace. After the death of Francesco on 25 October 1587, since there were no direct descendants, his brother, Cardinal Ferdinando, Cosimo's second son, was nominated Grand Duke of Tuscany. He resigned as cardinal and took on the title of Ferdinand I. In the late 16th century the new ruler decided to finish the construction begun by his father in Palazzo Vecchio, and created the building as we see it today, a building that covers a whole block and is bordered by Piazza della Signoria, Via dei Gondi, Via dei Leoni and Via della Ninna.

An unknown chronicler of the time gives the following description of the building in early 1588: "The Illustrious Cardinal and Grand Duke of Tuscany (Ferdinand I) decided to make an addition to the Palace in the Square at the back, in the area between that huge rusticated stone door designed by woodworker and architect Tasso and the corner of the palace, opposite Borgo dei Greci, at the corner of the street leading into the square; here there was nothing but an ugly old stretch of wall, about eight or ten *braccia* high, and the palace rooms behind that great door were visible to anyone passing by: one could see little balconies, terraces, gardens and other similar things. And between these rooms and that stretch of wall there was a huge empty space, with no building in it but a lot of rubbish; this was where the lions had originally been kept at the time of the Seigneury . . . So the Grand Duke commissioned from Bernardo Buontalenti, engineer and architect. . ."

But our documentary sources mention that the task of supervising the construction work was entrusted to the elderly Bartolomeo Ammannati (1511-1592), so it would appear that if the younger Bernardo Buontalenti (1536-1608) did actually oversee the project, it must have been after Ammannati's death in 1592, till the building was completed in 1596.

Ferdinand de' Medici was the last ruler of Tuscany who commissioned any work on the Palazzo Vecchio; as well as the construction work he commissioned from Ammannati, he also had several apartments restored and redecorated. But by the second half of the 16th century the Court had moved to the Pitti Palace, and that became the object of the sovereigns' attentions. From the late 16th century till the early 19th no further building or decorating operations were carried out on the Palazzo Vecchio, although it continued to be the seat of all major government offices. There were unfortunately several serious accidents, like a very bad fire: "On the 17 December 1690, on a Sunday at nine o'clock in the evening, a fire broke out in Palazzo Vecchio, caused by the carelessness of a woman who had put a hot coal bedwarmer in her bed and forgotten about it; very quickly a huge fire broke out and burned twenty-seven rooms between the Depository and the street that leads to the Salt Warehouse; the Royal Hall was miraculously spared, even though it was totally emptied of its furnishing for fear that the flames might reach it." This fire caused enormous damages, assessed at 120,000 *scudi*. On 12 July 1737, on the death of the last of the Medici, Gian Gastone, the Grand Duchy passed into the hands of the Lorraine family; but the new rulers never used the palace, not even Peter Leopold, an enlightened reformer and the promoter of important public works. He never spent a single *scudo* on Palazzo Vecchio, while he lavished huge sums on the Pitti Palace and the Boboli Gardens.

In 1792 a restoration project, commissioned by Grand Duke Ferdinand III, was begun. The contemporary chronicler Rastrelli witnessed these reconstruction operations and in his 1792 *Historical Illustration of the Palazzo della Signoria* he recalls: "It was truly important that such an illustrious monument of the Florentine nation not be lost to the passing of the centuries: and the heavens had reserved this glory to the age of the reign of Ferdinand III, by public vote nominated the Father of the People and of the Poor. He ordered that restoration work be begun, thereby saving those parts that were falling to ruin and bringing back to light the memories of the past and making it more beautiful. We can now see how it has been given a totally new form, for it has been rebuilt and replastered where necessary; the tower and the battlements have been coloured like stone; the inside window frames are in white marble, for the old ones were all crumbled and cracked, since they were made of stone like the rest of the building; the little terrace on the main facade has also been rebuilt, like the platform that surrounded the side facing the Corn Market; in the same way, the interior has been restored, and the Courtyard is being worked on at the moment, to restore it to its original condition." This restoration project, described in such detail by Rastrelli, was actually no more than an unsuccessful attempt at giving the Palazzo Vecchio the appearance of a Neoclassical building. Ferdinand III disappeared from the scene in 1796, with the arrival of Napoleon Bonaparte, commander in chief of the French army in Italy. In 1799 a new State, with a new Sovereign, the King of Etruria, was created; but this new kingdom did not last very long, for in 1807 Tuscany was annexed to the Napoleonic Empire.

The first mayor of Florence, elected by the government council in August 1808, was Cavalier Emilio Pucci; the executive board also nominated Giuseppe Del Rosso municipal

The corner on
Piazza San Firenze

architect. Among the important restoration works that Del Rosso supervised there were also several operations that concerned the Palazzo Vecchio, both in terms of the construction (he repaired the roof and the ceilings in several rooms) and of its decoration: he removed the plastering of the courtyard which consisted of a graffito pattern of gold fleur-de-lys. Del Rosso also had a door opened in the main facade of the palace, thus interrupting the Aringhiera, while he closed the door Vasari had put in between the courtyard and the Sala d'Arme.
It was not until 1814, after the fall of Napoleon, that the Grand Duchy was reinstated and Ferdinand III returned from his exile in Vienna. After Del Rosso, further restoration work in the Palazzo Vecchio was supervised by architect Giuseppe Martelli, who removed the stone-coloured plaster from the tower and the main facade that concealed the medieval rusticated stone facing. Between 1848 and 1860 Palazzo Vecchio witnessed all the political events that led eventually to Tuscany being annexed to the newborn Kingdom of Italy. From 1865 to 1871 Florence became the capital of Italy and Palazzo Vecchio was the seat of the government; before and during this period large sections of the palace underwent several transformations, including the two Council Halls, Sala dei Dugento and Salone dei Cinquecento, which were used as the Chamber of Deputies and the Senate of the Kingdom. In several instances earlier constructions were demolished. The projects and supervision of all work was entrusted to the Inspector of Civil

The northern facade with the windows of the Salone dei Cinquecento

Engineering and member of the Council for Public Works, Carlo Falconieri.
In 1872 Palazzo Vecchio became the property of the City of Florence and in September of that year the mayor, Ubaldino Peruzzi, took possession of his office. The municipality, although its financial situation was anything but florid, hired architect Emilio de Fabris to complete the section of the Salone dei Cinquecento near Via della Ninna; later he was also commissioned to supervise the restoration of the Apartments of Leo X, of the Elements (the Saturn terrace was reopened) and the walkway around the battlements, where the archways were opened up again; the Sala dei Dugento was rearranged and furnished with the tapestries we mentioned earlier and it became the hall where the City Council held its meetings; lastly, the partitions dividing the Dogana courtyard into many small rooms were removed.
In 1908 Alfredo Lensi, director of the Arts Department of the City Council of Florence, drew up a project for an overall restoration of the whole palace. Lensi's project was approved and a complex restoration that was to last for over twenty years began, opening to the public the Salone dei Cinquecento, the Apartments of the Elements and of Eleanor. Together with Giovanni Poggi, Lensi also entirely reconstructed Francesco I's Studiolo and arranged the Loeser Collection in the mezzanine. Since

The facade with the tower and the Commune's coats-of-arms below the corbel

this extensive restoration project Palazzo Vecchio has undergone several other important reconstructions, and many more are planned for the future: all are intended to help preserve a building which for the past seven hundred years has been the centre of the political and administrative life of the city, very closely connected to the history of Florence.

ART HISTORICAL GUIDE TO THE PALACE

by Alessandro Cecchi

Ground Floor

Plan of the Ground Floor
1. First Courtyard
2. Camera dell'Arme
3. Cortile della Dogana

FIRST COURTYARD

Facades (c1453). Architecture designed by Michelozzo di Bartolomeo (c1396-1472), who transformed the old 14th-century courtyard into a Renaissance structure, with two-light mullioned windows and oculi, originally decorated with graffito ashlars and gilded fleur-de-lys (a few examples of this decoration were brought to light during the 1973 restoration).

△
View of the first courtyard

Fountain (1555-1557). Made by Francesco Ferrucci called Il Tadda and Raffaello di Domenico di Polo (second half of the 16th century) according to designs by Giorgio Vasari (1511-1574) and perhaps Bartolomeo Ammannati. Today the statue of a *Putto with a Dolphin* by Andrea del Verrocchio (1435-1488) has been replaced by a copy; the original is on the Terrace of Juno inside the palace.

Ceilings of the Loggia (1565). Grotesque decorations by Marco da Faenza (1527?-1588), Stefano Veltroni and Orazio Porta from Monte San Savino (second half of the 16th century).

Columns (1565). Gilded stucco decoration by Pietro Paolo Minzocchi from Forlì, Leonardo Ricciarelli from Volterra, Lorenzo Marignolli (all active second half of the 16th century), Battista del Tadda from Fiesole (?-1617) and Santi Buglioni (1494-1576).

▷
Decoration of a column in the first courtyard

The fountain in the first courtyard

Side Walls (1565). Grotesque decorations by Marco da Faenza, Stefano Veltroni and Orazio Porta from Monte San Savino. Views of cities of the Austrian Empire by Bastiano Veronese, Giovanni Lombardi, Cesare Baglioni and Turino da Piemonte (second half of the 16th century); starting from the one to the left of the entrance from the square: *Prague*, *Passau*, *Stein*, *Klosterneuburg*, *Graz* (the best preserved) *Freyburg*, *Linz*, *Breslau*, *Vienna*, *Innsbruck*, *Ebersdorf*, *Konstanz*, *Neustadt*, *Hall*.

In the niche next to the arch leading to the Cortile della Dogana (c1550-54): Pierino da Vinci (1531-1554), *Samson Kills a Philistine*, a marble sculpture carved for Luca Martini and placed here in 1592. As Lensi pointed out, the Philistine is a portrait of Michelangelo Buonarroti.

View of the city of Graz in the first courtyard

CAMERA DELL'ARME
(before 1312)

This is the only part of the original Palazzo dei Priori that has survived unaltered, with its brick cross-vaulting and stone ribbing resting on stone pillars.

It was restored in 1910: the original plastering was removed and the door leading to the square, which had been walled up in 1380, was reopened.

CORTILE DELLA DOGANA

(1495-1496)

The Great Hall of the Council (later called Salone dei Cinquecento) was built above the courtyard, covered with a vaulted ceiling supported by huge pillars, on a project by Simone del Pollaiolo called Cronaca (1475-1508). The north door was built at the time of the Duke of Athens (1342-43), while the pediment on the outside dates from 1351.
In a passageway overlooking the south side of the courtyard, towards Via della Ninna, we can see the copper *pennant* (originally gilded), in the shape of a lion rampant holding the Florentine fleur-de-lys, which was placed at the top of the tower in August 1453. In 1981 it was removed and replaced by a copy in gilded fibreglass.
On the lefthand wall there are three stone *coats-of-arms* that still show traces of colouring and gilding; they date from the 14th and 15th centuries and belonged to three Captains of the People who, like the Podestà, could not by law be native Florentines. The one to the left, with lion claws on a gold and blue background, is the coat-of-arms of Ludovico di Tommaso di Ronco Sighifredo from Reggio, who was in office in 1433 when he was entrusted the task of arresting and taking into custody Cosimo the Elder.

The *Main Stairway*, covered by a barrel-vault, with handrails and pillars in pietra serena, was built between 1561 and 1565 on a project by Giorgio Vasari to replace the earlier one designed by Cronaca; it leads to the *First Floor*, to the *Salone dei Cinquecento*.

Pennant with the Marzocco lion and the Florentine fleur-de-lys formerly placed at the top of the tower

◁
Cortile della Dogana

Camera dell'Arme

Vasari's stairway

First Floor

Ground-plan of the First Floor
1. Salone dei Cinquecento
2. Francesco I's Studiolo

Apartment of Leo X
3. Room of Leo X
4. Room of Cosimo the Elder
5. Room of Lorenzo the Magnificent
6. Room of Cosimo I
7. Room of Giovanni dalle Bande Nere
8. Private study
9. Chapel
10. Room of Clement VII
11. Sala dei Dugento

SALONE DEI CINQUECENTO

On the north wall, to the left of the entrance: "*Udienza*" (1542/43?-1595). Architecture designed by Giuliano Baccio d'Agnolo (1491-1555), completed with decorations by Giorgio Vasari and assistants. Sculptures by Baccio Bandinelli (1488-1560), Vincenzo de' Rossi (1525-1587) and Giovanni Caccini (1566-1612/13).

From left to right:
Cosimo I (1519-1574), by Baccio Bandinelli, finished by Vincenzo de' Rossi. Above: Cosimo's emblem, a tortoise and a sail.
Giovanni dalle Bande Nere (1498-1526), by Baccio Bandinelli. Above: Giovanni's emblem, a bolt of lightning.
Leo X (1475-1521), by Baccio Bandinelli, finished by Vincenzo de' Rossi. Above: the Pope's emblem, a yoke with the motto "Enim Suave."
Alessandro de' Medici (1511-1537), by Baccio Bandinelli. Above: the Duke's emblem, a rhinoceros.

The Salone dei Cinquecento

The "Udienza" in the Salone dei Cinquecento

Baccio Bandinelli
Statue of Cosimo I

Clement VII (1478-1534), by Baccio Bandinelli, shown crowning *Charles V Hapsburg* (1500-1558), by Giovanni Caccini.
Francesco I (1541-1587), by Giovanni Caccini. Above: his emblem, a weasel with the motto "Amat Victoria curam."

Ceiling (1563-1565)
The ceiling of the Republican Council Hall (1495-96) was raised by twelve *braccia* (about twenty feet) to its present height, and the room was given a new ceiling by Bernardo d'Antonio di Monna Mattea (second half of the 16th century); carpentry and wood inlay work by Battista di Bartolomeo Botticelli (second half of the 16th century) and assistants. The paintings, following an iconographical programme drawn up by Don Vincenzo Borghini (1515-1580) and a project by Giorgio Vasari, were painted by Vasari himself, by the Flemish-born Jan van der Straet, called Giovanni Stradano (1523-1605), Jacopo Zucchi (c1541-c1589) and Giovan Battista Naldini (c1537-1591); the were assisted by Stefano Veltroni, Tommaso di Battista del Verrocchio (second half of the 16th century), Prospero Fontana (1512-1597), Marco Marchetti from Faenza (1527?-1588), Orazio Porta from Monte San Savino, Santi di Tito (1536-1603) and Michele di Ridolfo del Ghirlandaio (1503-1577).
The allegorical programme of the paintings is intended as a glorification of Florence, through the famous events of its history and its territorial and administrative subdivisions; but the place of honour, in the roundel in the middle, is dedicated to the apotheosis of Cosimo I de' Medici, being crowned by "Fiorenza." Cosimo, the founder of the Ducal State, had won the war against Siena in only fifteen months (1554-55), whereas the Florentine Republic had had to fight for fourteen years (1496-1509) in order to defeat Pisa.

Starting from the left, above the north wall, moving towards the right:
In the middle of the double corner: *Putti on a balustrade with a ball, a mask and sticks* .
Portraits of Bernardo di Monna Mattea, Battista Botticelli, Stefano Veltroni and Marco da Faenza, Vasari's assistants.
Putti with a scroll and a Latin inscription celebrating the completion of the ceiling in 1565.
Allegory of Prato; *Allegory of Pistoia*; *Allegory*

The stuccoes in the Salone dei Cinquecento showing Medici heraldic devices.

From left to right: devices of Cosimo I, of Giovanni dalle Bande Nere, of Alessandro de' Medici, of Francesco de' Medici and of Leo X

G. Vasari and assistants
Portraits of Bernardo di Monna Mattea, Battista Botticelli, Stefano Veltroni and Marco da Faenza

◁
G. Vasari and assistants
Ceiling of the Salone dei Cinquecento, detail of the central section

G. Vasari and assistants
Ceiling of the Salone dei Cinquecento, *Allegory of the city of Pistoia*

of Pescia; *Allegory of San Miniato in the lower Arno valley*.
Roundel: *Allegory of the city quarters of Santa Maria Novella and of San Giovanni with their Banners*.
Allegory of Fiesole; *Allegory of Romagna*; *Allegory of Mugello*; *Allegory of Casentino*.

Along the wall opposite the Stairway there are seven panels illustrating the war against Siena (1554-55). From left to right: *The Capture of Monastero*; *Cosimo I Studies Plans for the Capture of Siena*; *The Capture of Casole*; *Triumph after the Fall of Siena*; *The Capture of Monteriggioni*; *The Battle of Marciano in the Chiana Valley*; *Defeat of the Turks at Piombino*.

Along the central axis of the ceiling there are panels glorifying Florence and Cosimo I de' Medici. From left to right:
Defeat of Radagasius at the Foot of Fiesole; *Foundation of the Roman Colony of Florence*; *Clement IV Gives his Banner to the Captains of the Guelphs*; *Apotheosis of Cosimo I*; *Eugene IV Lands in Livorno to Seek Shelter in Florence*; *Arnolfo Illustrates to the Priors his Plan for the En-*

largement of Florence and the New Set of City Walls; *Florence and Fiesole Unite*.

Along the wall above the entrance from the Main Stairway there are seven panels illustrating episodes from the war against Pisa.
From left to right:
The Capture of Cascina; *Antonio Giacomini Addresses the People*; *The Capture of Vicopisano*; *Triumph after the Victory over Pisa*; *The Battle of Barbagianni, near Pisa*; *The Venetians are Defeated in the Casentino; Naval Battle between Florence and Pisa*.
Along the southern wall, from left to right:
Allegory of Cortona and Montepulciano; *Allegory of Arezzo*; *Allegory of Borgo San Sepolcro and Anghiari*; *Allegory of San Giovanni Valdarno*.
Roundel: *Allegory of the city quarters of Santa Croce and Santo Spirito with their Banners*.
Allegory of Volterra; *Allegory of Colle Val d'Elsa and San Gimignano*; *Allegory of Certaldo*; *Allegory of the Chianti*.

The Genius of Victory
At the centre of the wall opposite the Stairway stands the *Genius of Victory* by Michelangelo Buonarroti (1475-1564), carved in 1533-34 for the tomb of Julius II. It was placed here in

G. Vasari and assistants
Ceiling of the Salone dei Cinquecento, *Cosimo I Plans the Conquest of Siena*

G. Vasari and assistants
Ceiling of the Salone dei Cinquecento, *Defeat of Radagasius at the Foot of Fiesole*

G. Vasari and assistants
Ceiling of the Salone dei Cinquecento, *Triumph after the Fall of Siena*; below right: portraits of Vasari and his assistants

G. Vasari and assistants
Ceiling of the Salone dei Cinquecento, *Apotheosis of Cosimo I*

G. Vasari and assistants
Ceiling of the Salone dei Cinquecento,
Arnolfo Illustrates to the Priors his Plan for the Enlargement of Florence

G. Vasari and assistants
Ceiling of the Salone dei Cinquecento,
Antonio Giacomini Addresses the People

G. Vasari and assistants
Ceiling of the Salone dei Cinquecento, *Allegory of San Giovanni Valdarno*

G. Vasari and assistants
Ceiling of the Salone dei Cinquecento, *Allegory of the City Quarters of Santa Croce and Santo Spirito with their Banners*

▷
Michelangelo
The Genius of Victory
(Salone dei Cinquecento)

G. Vasari and assistants
Ceiling of the Salone dei Cinquecento, *The Capture of Cascina*

The wooden structure of the ceiling of the Salone dei Cinquecento

1565; although it was later removed, it returned to its original place in 1980, on the occasion of the Medici Exhibition.

Walls (1567-1571)
Frescoes of episodes from the wars against Siena and Pisa by Giorgio Vasari, Giovan Battista Naldini, Jacopo Zucchi, Giovanni Stradano (Jan van der Straet) and assistants.

On the wall opposite the entrance from the Stairway, from left to right, three episodes from the war against Siena (1554-55):
The Capture of the Fort near the Camollia Gate in Siena; *The Capture of Porto Ercole*; *The Battle of Marciano in Val di Chiana.*

On the entrance wall, from left to right, three episodes from the war against Pisa (1496-1509):
Defeat of the Pisans at Torre di San Vincenzo; *Emperor Maximilian Lifts his Siege of Livorno*; *The Capture of the Fortress of Stampace at Pisa.*

In the middle of the entrance wall, to the left of the Stairway, there is a life-size plaster model of the statue of *Florence Defeating Pisa* by the Flemish-born Giambologna (1529-1608); the model was placed here in 1565, replaced probably in 1589 by the statue itself, which today is in the Bargello National Museum. The model was brought back in 1980, for the Medici Show.

Above, on either side of the "Udienza" on the north wall, two paintings on slate by the Veronese Jacopo Ligozzi (1547-1626), dating from 1590-92; Ligozzi was helped by his cousin Francesco di Mercurio (second half of the 16th century), Donato Mascagni (1579-1636) and others.

Left: *Boniface VIII Receives the Twelve Floren-*

△
G. Vasari and assistants
The Capture of the Fort near the Camollia Gate in Siena
(Salone dei Cinquecento, east wall)

▽
G. Vasari and assistants
Defeat of the Pisans at Torre di San Vicenzo
(Salone dei Cinquecento, west wall)

Jacopo Ligozzi
Boniface VIII Receives the Twelve Florentine Ambassadors Representing the Major Powers
(Salone dei Cinquecento, west wall, above the "Udienza")

tine Ambassadors Representing the Powers of Europe and Asia (1295).

Right: *Cosimo de' Medici is Crowned Grand Duke of Tuscany by Pope Pius V* (1569).

Above, on either side of the architectural facade of the south wall, two paintings on slate by Domenico Cresti called Passignano (c1560-1636) and assistants, dating from 1597-99.
Left: *Pius IV Nominates Duke Cosimo de' Medici Grand Master of the Order of St Stephen* (1562).

Right: *Cosimo de' Medici is Nominated Duke of Florence by the Florentine Senate* (1537).

Along the walls:
Statues of *The Labours of Hercules* by Vincenzo de' Rossi and assistants, dating from 1562-84; there were seven statues, but one of them, Hercules Carrying Atlas's Globe, was removed in the 17th century and now stands next to the entrance to the Villa of Poggio Imperiale. The other six were placed here in 1592.

South wall (1882) The architectural decoration designed by Bartolomeo Ammannati between 1588 and 1591 was altered by Emilio de Fabris (1808-1883) who placed a large statue of *Savonarola* in the central niche; the statue has now been transferred to the square dedicated to Savonarola. In 1921 it was replaced by Michelangelo's *Genius of Victory*, which was then moved in 1980 to the wall opposite the entrance. In the side niches there are Roman copies of Greek originals: *Pothos*, *Mercury*, *Apollo* and *Bacchus*.

V. De Rossi
Hercules and the Centaur (Salone dei Cinquecento)

V. De Rossi
Hercules Strangles Antaeus (Salone dei Cinquecento)

STUDIOLO
(1570-1575)

To the right of the south wall, through a passageway created in the 19th century (when Florence was the capital of Italy and the Salone dei Cinquecento was used as the Chamber of Deputies), one can look into the *"Studiolo"* of Francesco I de' Medici, rearranged in 1910 according to the reconstruction by Alfredo Lensi and Giovanni Poggi.

This small room may originally have been used by Duke Cosimo as a vault for his strongbox, the door of which was carved by Vincenzo Danti (1530-1576) and is now in the Bargello. The Prince Regent Francesco turned the room into a container "of rare and precious objects, of valuables and works of art"; the decoration of the room, an iconographical programme drawn up by Don Vincenzo Borghini, illustrates the close relationship between Nature and Art. Borghini's programme was transformed into a figurative project by Giorgio Vasari, who was assisted by several painters and sculptors as well as the wood-carver Dionigi di Matteo Nigetti (doc. from 1560 to 1600). The authors of the paintings are:
Francesco Morandini called Poppi (1544-1579), Jacopo Zucchi, Alessandro Allori (1535-1607), Niccolò Betti (?-post 1617), Ludovico Buti (active 1560-1590), Giovan Maria Butteri (c1540-1606), Vittore Casini (active

A. Allori (after Bronzino)
Portrait of Cosimo I
(Studiolo)

A. Allori (after Bronzino)
Portrait of Eleanor of Toledo (Studiolo)

View of the Studiolo

G. Vasari
Perseus and Andromeda (Studiolo)

1567-1572), Mirabello Cavalori (1510/20-1572), Jacopo Coppi (1523-1591), Francesco Coscia (active c1570-1590), Giovanni Fedini (active c1565-1582), Alessandro Fei (1543-1592), Girolamo Macchietti (1539/41-1592), Sebastiano Marsili (active c1570), Tommaso Manzuoli called Maso da San Friano (1531-1571), Andrea del Minga (?-1596), Giovan Battista Naldini, Carlo Portelli (before 1510-1574), Santi di Tito, Lorenzo dello Sciorina (1540/50-1598), Giovanni Stradano, Bartolomeo Traballesi (?-1585).
The authors of the sculptures are:
Bartolomeo Ammannati, Giovanni Bandini

Santi di Tito
Phaeton's Sisters (Studiolo)

Maso da San Friano
The Diamond Mine
(Studiolo)

G. B. Naldini
Gathering Ambergris (Studiolo)

G. Stradano
The Alchemist's Laboratory (Studiolo)

Giambologna
Apollo (Studiolo)

B. Ammannati
Opi (Studiolo)

(1540-1599), Elia Candido (1548-1628), Vincenzo Danti, Giambologna, Stoldo Lorenzi (1534-1583), Domenico Poggini (1520-1590), Vincenzo de' Rossi.

On the ceiling, in the middle: *Nature and Prometheus* (F. Poppi); at the sides, the Four Elements, *Fire*, *Water*, *Air* (F. Poppi) and *Earth* (J. Zucchi); in the other panels there are the links between the Elements, symbolized by pairs of putti, *Dry*, *Cold*, *Humid* and *Hot* (J. Zucchi) and the Humours of Man, *Melancholy*, *Phlegm* (J. Zucchi), *Blood* and *Rage* (F. Poppi).

In the lunettes, round portraits of the Prince's parents, *Cosimo de' Medici* and *Eleanor of Toledo* (by A. Allori after Bronzino).

On the walls, from left to right and from top to bottom, starting from the passageway leading to the Salone dei Cinquecento:
Statuette of Amphitrite (S. Lorenzi), *Perseus Frees Andromeda* (G. Vasari), *The Crossing of the Red Sea* (S. di Tito), *Gathering Ambergris* (G. B. Naldini), *Phaeton's Sisters Turned into Poplars* (S. di Tito), *The Wool Mill* (M. Cavalori), *Pearl Fishing* (A. Allori), *Statuette of*

Venus (V. Danti); below: *Alexander Presents Campaspe to Apelles* (F. Poppi), *Neptune and Amphitrite* (C. Portelli), *Lavinia at the Altar* (M. Cavalori), *Ulysses, Mercury and Circe* (G. Stradano), *Allegory of Dreams* (G. B. Naldini), *Cleopatra's Banquet* (A. Allori), *Juno Borrows Venus's Girdle* (F. Cossia).

On the upper part of the end wall: *Statuette of Juno* (G. Bandini), *The Diamond Mine* (M. da San Friano), *Statuette of Aeolus* (E. Candido); in the lower part: *Aeneas Lands in Italy* (G. M. Butteri), *The Fall of Icarus* (M. da San Friano).

On the upper part of the righthand wall: *Statuette of Apollo* (Giambologna), *Hot Springs at Pozzuoli* (G. Macchietti), *The Invention of Gun Powder* (J. Coppi), *Glassworks* (G. M. Butteri), *The Goldsmith's Workshop* (A. Fei), *The Alchemist's Laboratory* (G. Stradano), *The Foundry* (F. Poppi), *Statuette of Vulcan* (V. de' Rossi); on the lower level: *The Ring of Polycrates, King of Samos* (G. Fedini), *Medea Rejuvenates Aeson* (G. Macchietti), *Hercules Slays the Dragon of the Hesperides* (L. dello Sciorina), *Hercules and Iole* (S. di Tito), *Plunder* (N. Betti), *Apollo and Chiron* (L. Buti), *The Family of Darius before Alexander* (J. Coppi), *Vulcan's Forge* (V. Casini).

On the upper part of the entrance wall: *Statuette of Pluto* (D. Poggini), *The Gold Mine* (J. Zucchi), *Statuette of Opi* (B. Ammannati); on the lower level: *Danae* (B. Traballesi), *Deucalion and Pyrrha* (A. del Minga), *Atalanta* (S. Marsili).

APARTMENT OF LEO X

On the lefthand side of the south wall, opposite the passageway leading to the "Studiolo," is the entrance to the *Apartment of Leo X*, named after the large room that almost all the other rooms open onto; each room is named after a famous member of the Medici family. There is also a small chapel in the Apartment. In the 16th century this Apartment was used as the official reception area; recently (1982-84) these rooms have been restored to their original splendour, with their precious gilded stucco paintings, frames and mouldings in pietra serena or coloured marble, counterbalanced by the lovely floors in red and white terracotta tiles (which will soon be restored).

The complex programme of the decorations was drawn up by the learned Cosimo Bartoli (1503-1572) and it was executed by Court painter and architect Giorgio Vasari, assisted by master mason Bernardo d'Antonio di Monna Mattea, woodcarvers Antonio di Rombolo called Crocino and Domenico del Tasso, gilder Mariotto di Francesco (second half of the 16th century), sculptors Bartolomeo Ammannati and Antonio di Gino Lorenzi (?-1583), stuccoworkers Leonardo Ricciarelli and Giovanni di Tommaso Boscoli (1524-1589), and painters Marco da Faenza and Giovanni Stradano, as well as other minor assistants. The floor tiles, in red and white terracotta, were made by Santi di Michele Buglioni (1494-1576) and assistants.

Work on the Apartment took place between 1555 and 1562 and the last rooms to be finished were those of Leo X and Clement VII.

Room of Leo X

This room is named after Cardinal Giovanni de' Medici (1475-1521), the son of Lorenzo the Magnificent, who was elected Pope in 1513.

Ceiling. In the centre is *The Capture of Milan Occupied by the French* (1521); in the side panels, beginning with the one above the door leading to the Salone dei Cinquecento, from left to right: *Giuliano, Leo X's brother, is granted Roman citizenship* (1513); *Cardinal Giulio de' Medici is sent as Leo X's ambassador to Lombardy* (1521); *Leo X meets Francis I in Bologna* (1515); *Cardinal Giovanni de' Medici, prisoner of the French, watches the battle of Ravenna* (1512); *Cardinal Giovanni de' Medici escapes capture* (1512); *Cardinal Giovanni de' Medici returns to Florence* (1512); *Lorenzo, the nephew of Leo X, is made Duke of Urbino* (1516); *Giovanni de' Medici is elected Pope* (1513).

Side walls. On the wall to the left of the entrance, within stucco niches, are the busts of *Giuliano, Duke of Nemours* (1479-1516) by Alfonso Lombardi (1497-1537) and *Lorenzo, Duke of Urbino* (1492-1519) by Antonio di Gino Lorenzi. Between them is *The Capture of San Leo* (1517) and, below, *Bramante presents the ground plan of St Peter's to Leo X* (1513-14).

On the wall opposite are the busts of *Clement VII* (1478-1534) by Alfonso Lombardi and of *Leo X* (1475-1521) by Antonio di Gino Lorenzi; between them, the fresco of *Leo X electing a group of cardinals* (1517) and, below, an original fireplace designed by Ammannati.
On the wall with the windows, from left to right: on the upper level, within ovals, the portraits of *Marguerite of Austria* (1522-1586), the wife of Alessandro de' Medici, and of *Eleanor of Toledo* (1522-1562), the wife of Duke Cosimo de' Medici; in the roundels above the windows, the portraits of *Cardinal Giovanni de' Medici* (1543-1562), the son of Cosimo I, of *Catherine de' Medici* (1519-1589), the daughter of Lorenzo, Duke of Urbino, and of *Cardinal Ippolito de' Medici* (1511-1535), illegitimate son of Giuliano, Duke of Nemours. In the

G. Vasari and assistants
The ceiling of the Room of Leo X

△
G. Vasari and assistants
The Room of Leo X

▽
G. Vasari
The Entrance of Leo X into Florence (Room of Leo X)

panels between the windows there are the full-length portraits, in ancient costumes, of *Duke Alessandro de' Medici* (1511-1537), with the *Foundation of the Fortezza da Basso* (1533) below, and of *Duke Cosimo de' Medici* (1519-1574), with the *Construction of the Fortress of Siena* (1561) below.
On the wall nearest the Salone dei Cinquecento, *The Solemn Entrance of Leo X into Florence* (1515) and, below it, *Leo X Sends his Cap and his Sword as a Gift to Florence* (1513?). The white and red terracotta tiles are arranged so as to repeat the divisions of the ceiling.

The other rooms of this Apartment are presently used as administrative offices and are not open to the public.

The Room of Cosimo the Elder

This room is named after the founder (1389-1464) of the Medici wealth and power in the Quattrocento.

Ceiling. In the middle of the ceiling, *Cosimo the Elder Returns from Exile* (1434); at the sides, framed by stucco mouldings and niches designed by Ammannati, episodes from his life and allegorical representations.

From left to right, beginning from the one above the entrance door (from the Salone dei Cinquecento): *Cosimo Surrounded by Artists and Men of Letters*, between the *Allegories of Eternity and Fame*; below the main scene, *Portrait of Lorenzo de' Medici* (1395-1440), Cosimo's brother. The next panel shows *Cosimo Exiled from Florence* (1433), between the *Allegories of Fortitude and Prudence*; below the main scene, *Portrait of Piero de' Medici, called Piero the Gouty* (1416-1469), Cosimo's son. The next panel shows *Cosimo Reveals to Santi Bentivoglio his Origins* so that he may rule Bologna (1446), between the *Allegories of Cunning and Courage*; below the main scene, *Portrait of Giovanni, called Bicci, de' Medici* (1360-1429), Cosimo's father. In the last panel of the ceiling, *Brunelleschi and Ghiberti Present to Cosimo their Model of the Church of San Lorenzo* (after 1421), between the *Allegories of Diligence and Religion*; below the main scene, *Portrait of Giovanni de' Medici* (1421-1463), Cosimo's second son.

Side walls. Grotesque decorations.

G. Vasari
Cosimo the Elder Returns from Exile (Room of Cosimo the Elder)

G. Vasari and assistants: The Room of Cosimo the Elder

G. Vasari and Marco da Faenza *Brunelleschi and Ghiberti Present to Cosimo their Model of the Church of San Lorenzo* (Room of Cosimo the Elder)

Marco da Faenza
Oval panel showing the enlargement and restoration of the Monastery of San Marco (Room of Cosimo the Elder)

Room of Lorenzo the Magnificent

This room is named after the greatest statesman and patron of the arts of the Medici dynasty: Lorenzo (1449-1492), who was the son of Piero the Gouty.

Ceiling. In the middle, *Lorenzo the Magnificent Receives the Ambassadors of the major powers of his times;* at the sides, beginning from the panel above the entrance door (from the Room of Cosimo the Elder), from left to right: *The Capture of Sarzana* (1487), between the *Allegories of Clemency and Good Judgment;* below the main scene, *Portrait of Giovanni de' Medici* (1475-1521), Lorenzo's son who later became Pope Leo X. The next panel shows *Lorenzo de' Medici at the Diet of Cremona* (1483), between the *Allegories of Fearlessness* (Hercules slaying the Hydra) *and of Glad Tidings;* below the main scene, *Portrait of Giuliano de' Medici* (1479-1516), Lorenzo's youngest son. The next panel shows *Lorenzo in Naples Visiting King Ferdinand of Aragon* (1479-80), between the *Allegories of Faith and Compassion;* below the main scene, *Portrait of Piero de' Medici* (1472-

G. Vasari and assistants
The Room of Lorenzo the Magnificent

G. Vasari and assistants
Lorenzo the Magnificent Receives the Ambassadors (Ceiling of the Room of Lorenzo the Magnificent)

G. Vasari and assistants
Lorenzo the Magnificent Surrounded by the Philosophers and Men of Letters of his Time (Room of Lorenzo the Magnificent)

1503), called Piero the Foolish, Lorenzo's second son. In the last panel of the ceiling, *Lorenzo Surrounded by Philosophers and Men of Letters,* between the *Allegories of Fame and Virtue;* below the main scene, *Portrait of Giuliano de' Medici* (1453-1478), Lorenzo's younger brother killed in the Pazzi Conspiracy.

Side walls: Grotesque decorations.

Room of Cosimo I

This room is named after the founder (1519-1574) of the Medici ducal State in the 16th century, a patron of the arts who commissioned the modernization of the palace.

Ceiling. In the middle, *Cosimo's Victory at Montemurlo* (1537); at the sides, beginning from the panel above the entrance door (from the Room of Leo X), from left to right: *Cosimo de' Medici is Elected Duke of Florence* (1537), between the *Allegories of Pistoia and Prato*; below, the *Double Portrait of Don Giovanni* (1543-1562) *and Don Garzia de' Medici* (1547-1562), two of Cosimo's sons, and *Views of Piombino and Livorno*. The next panels shows *Cosimo amongst the Artists of his Court*, between the *Allegories of Fivizzano and Volterra*; below, *Portrait of Francesco de' Medici* (1541-1587), Cosimo's eldest son, and *Views of Empoli and Lucignano*. The next panel shows *Cosimo Sending Reinforcements to Serravalle* (1554), between the *Allegories of Cortona and Borgo San Sepolcro*; below, *Portrait of Pietro de' Medici* (1554-1604), son of Cosimo, and *Views of Montecarlo and Scarperia*. In the last panel of the ceiling,

G. Vasari and assistants
Portrait of Don Giovanni and Don Garzia de' Medici (Ceiling of the Room of Cosimo I)

G. Vasari and assistants: Ceiling of the Room of Cosimo I

G. Vasari and assistants
Cosimo with his Architects (Ceiling of the Room of Cosimo I)

G. Vasari and assistants
Cosimo I amongst the Artists of his Court (Ceiling of the Room of Cosimo I)

G. Vasari and G. Stradano
The Birth of Francesco I
(Room of Cosimo I)

G. Vasari and G. Stradano
Eleanor of Toledo Arrives at Poggio a Caiano
(Room of Cosimo I)

Cosimo Inspecting the Fortifications on the Island of Elba (1548), between the *Allegories of Arezzo and Pisa*; below, *Portrait of Eleanor of Toledo* (1522-1562), Cosimo's wife, and *Views of Florence and Siena*.

Side walls. Beginning from the wall adjoining the Room of Leo X, and moving from left to right: *The Baptism of Francesco I* (1541), *The Capture of Porto Ercole* (1555), *Restoration of the Castle of Florence* (1543); on the following wall, *Francesco de' Medici Visits Spain* (or *Cosimo Meets the Emperor in Genoa*) (1543), *The Defeat of the Turks at Piombino* (1555), *Duke Cosimo Receives the Order of the Golden Fleece in the Cathedral* (1545); on the following wall, *Cosimo I Enters Siena* (1557) and *The Birth of Francesco I* (1541); on the last wall, *Eleanor of Toledo Leaves Naples* (1539), *The Route of Valdichiana* (1554), *Eleanor of Toledo Arrives at Poggio a Caiano* (1539). All scenes are surrounded by grotesque decorations.

The red and white terracotta tiling on the floor repeats symmetrically the divisions of the ceiling.

Room of Giovanni dalle Bande Nere

This room is named after the famous Medici condottiero (1498-1526), the father of Cosimo I.

Ceiling. In the middle, *Giovanni and his Armies Cross the Rivers Po and Adda* (1521); at the sides, beginning from the panel above the entrance door (from the Room of Cosimo I), *The Battle of San Secondo* (1519), between the *Allegories of Honour and Courage* (?); below, *Portrait of Giovanni dalle Bande Nere* (1498-1526), between two bolts of lightning, the heraldic devices of the condottiero. Continuing, from left to right, we find *Giovanni Defending the Ponte Rozzo Bridge on the River Ticino* (1524), between the *Allegories of Fearlessness and Fortitude*; below, *Portrait of Maria Salviati* (1499-1545), Giovanni's wife, also surrounded by his heraldic devices. In the following panel, *Giovanni dalle Bande Nere Slays a Spanish Knight* (1526), between the *Allegories of Impetus and Fury*; below, *Portrait of Giovanni di Pierfrancesco de' Medici, called Il Popolano*

G. Vasari and assistants
Ceiling of the Room of Giovanni dalle Bande Nere

G. Vasari and assistants
Battle Scene (Room of Giovanni dalle Bande Nere)

G. Vasari
Julius Caesar Writes his Commentaries (Ceiling of the private study adjoining the Room of Giovanni dalle Bande Nere)

(1467-1498), Giovanni's father, again shown with the bolts of lightning. The last panel shows *The Capture of Caravaggio* (1524), between the *Allegories of Military Valour and Fortune*; below, *Portrait of Cosimo de' Medici as a Youth* (1519-1574), with his father's heraldic devices.

Side walls. Beginning from the wall adjoining the Room of Cosimo I, from left to right: *The Capture of Milan* (1521), *Portrait of Caterina Sforza* (1462-1509), Giovanni dalle Bande Nere's mother, *The Siege of a Fortified City,* near a bridge; on the following wall, *Armies on the March*, *The Siege of a Fortified Palace on Fire,* near a city with towers; on the following wall, two unidentifiable *Battles* among the many fought by the Medici general; on the last wall, *Skirmish between Giovanni and the Orsini family on the Sant'Angelo Bridge in Rome* (1525), *Portrait of Pierfrancesco de' Medici* (1430-1476), the father of Giovanni il Popolano, and the *Battle of Pontevico* (?).
All the scenes are framed by grotesque friezes.

G. Vasari and assistants
Room of Giovanni dalle Bande Nere

Private study adjoining the Room of Giovanni dalle Bande Nere

In an oval panel in the ceiling, *Julius Caesar Writes his Commentaries*, a reference to the military glories of Cosimo I de' Medici, who won the war against Siena.
Originally this room contained cupboards, writing desks, a window and a red and white terracotta tiled floor.

The Chapel of the Apartment of Leo X

The Chapel can be reached from several of the rooms of the Apartment; it is dedicated to Saints Cosma and Damian.

Ceiling. In an oval panel in the middle, *God the Father in Glory*; in the side panels, *Prophets and Sybils* (?), and in the roundels, *Sacrificial Offerings*; in the four spandrels, *Allegories of Charity*, *Justice*, *Hope* (?) and *Faith*.

Side walls. Beginning from the wall adjoining the Room of Leo X: above, in the lunette, *Sacrificial Offering*; below, from left to right, *St Luke*, *Manna Falling from Heaven*, *St Mark*, and, below still, *The Sermon of John the Baptist*, and in a roundel, *John the Baptist's Severed Head in a Bowl*. On the lefthand wall: above, in the lunette, *Sacrificial Offering*; below, from left to right, *St John*, *The Last Supper*, *St Matthew* and, below still, *The Baptism of Christ*. On the wall opposite: above, in the lunette, *Sacrifi-*

Unknown 16th-century artist
Copy of Raphael's *Madonna dell'Impannata*

On either side: G. Vasari
Saints Cosma and Damian (Chapel of the Apartment of Leo X)

Marco da Faenza
Baptism of Christ
(Chapel of the
Apartment of Leo X)

cial Offering; below, in the middle, 16th-century copy of Raphael's *Madonna dell'Impannata* (the original, which hung here in the 16th century, was painted for Bindo Altoviti around 1514); on either side, *Duke Cosimo as St Damian* and *Cosimo the Elder as St Cosma*; below the main scene, *Mater Dolorosa, Man of Sorrows between Two Angels*, and *Mary Magdalene*; below, two unidentified *Saints*. On the last wall, the righthand wall: above, *Sacrificial Offering*; below, *St John the Baptist*, *The Beheading of John the Baptist* and *John the Baptist in Prison*.
The coloured floor is still the original one; like those in the other rooms, it repeats the divisions of the ceiling.

Ceiling of the Room of Clement VII

G. Vasari and assistants
Clement VII Nominates Ippolito de' Medici Cardinal (Room of Clement VII)

Room of Clement VII

This room is named after the other great Medici Pope (1478-1534), who continued the work of Leo X.

Ceiling. In the central panel, *Clement VII Crowns Charles V Hapsburg in San Petronio in Bologna* (1530); at the sides, beginning from the section above the entrance, from left to right: *Clement VII Returns to Rome from France* (1526), between the *Allegories of Fortune and Constancy*; in the frieze, two of Clement VII's heraldic devices (the sun with a crystal ball setting fire to a tree trunk, with the motto "Candor Illaesus"). On the next section of the ceiling, in the middle, *Ippolito de' Medici Is Sent to Hungary as Clement VII's Ambassador* (1532); to the left, *Allegory of Honour* and, in an oval, *Clement VII Nominates his Nephew Ippolito de' Medici Cardinal* (1529); to the right, in an oval, *Clement VII Opens the Holy Door for the 1525 Jubilee*, and *Allegory of Magnanimity*. In the next section, *Catherine de' Medici and Henry II of France Are Married in Marseilles* (1533), between the *Allegories of Wisdom (?) and Security*; in the frieze, two heraldic devices of Clement VII. On the long side of the ceiling, in

G. Vasari and G. Stradano
The Siege of Florence (Room of Clement VII)

the middle, *After his Imperial Nomination Duke Alessandro de' Medici Returns to Florence* (1532); to the left, *Allegory of Victory* and, in an oval, *Emperor Charles V Crowns Alessandro de' Medici Duke of Florence*; to the right, in an oval, *Alessandro de' Medici Marries Marguerite of Austria, Charles V's Daughter* (1536), and *Allegory of Fortitude*.

Side walls. Episodes from the 1529-30 war. Beginning from the entrance wall, from left to right: *The Armies, under the Command of Francesco Ferrucci's, March through Pisa*; *Clement VII with Francis I*; *The Orange Troops Battle with Ferrucci'Republican Army at Gavinana*. On the following wall: *The Camp near Pistoia*; *The Siege of Florence*; *Clement VII and Charles V*; *The Castle at Lastra a Signa on Fire*. On the next wall, *The Siege of the Castle at Empoli* and a *Skirmish in front of the Fort of San Giorgio*. On the last wall: *Battle outside the Porta Romana, near Marignolle*; *Philibert of Orange's Troops Camp near Volterra*; *Sally on the Plain near San Donato in Polverosa*. The white and red terracotta tiled floor follows the symmetry of the ceiling.

Up two very steep flights of steps, from the Room of Leo X, we reach the second floor. On the wall of the first landing, a fresco showing *The Firework Display on the Occasion of the Feast Day of John the Baptist* (G. Stradano); the barrel-vaulted ceiling of the stairway is decorated with grotesques by Marco da Faenza, with panels depicting flying putti and heraldic devices of Cosimo I (the crossed anchors with the motto "Duabus," the Capricorn, the Duke's sign of the zodiac, and the tortoise with the sail) or the attributes of ducal authority (the ducal crown, the six balls of the Medici coat-of-arms, the Imperial Order of the Golden Fleece).

Marco da Faenza
Grotesque decorations on the vaulted ceiling of the first landing

△
Marco da Faenza
Decoration of the vaulted ceiling of the second landing

The stairway leading up to the second floor

Second Floor

Ground-plan of the Second Floor

Apartment of the Elements
1. Room of the Elements
2. Room of Ceres
3. The Calliope Study
4. Room of Opi
5. Room of Jove
6. Terrace of Juno
7. Room of Hercules
8. The Minerva Study
9. Terrace of Saturn
10. The rooms of the Rodolfo Siviero Collection

Apartment of Eleanor
11. Green Room
12. Eleanor's Private Study
13. Eleanor's Chapel
14. Room of the Sabine Women
15. Room of Esther
16. Room of Penelope
17. Room of Gualdrada
18. Chapel of the Priors
19. Sala dell'Udienza
20. Sala dei Gigli
21. Chancery
22. Sala delle Carte Geografiche
23. Salotta

APARTMENT OF THE ELEMENTS

We reach this Apartment by climbing up the *Main Stairway* from the Apartment of Leo X. The architectural construction, including the Terrace of Saturn and the wooden loft in the Room of the Elements, as well as the design of all the other lofts, is the work of Battista del Tasso (1500-1555), master carpenter and palace architect before Vasari. The decoration of the Apartment, designed and supervised by Giorgio Vasari, was carried out between 1555

and 1558, except for the room known as the Minerva Study and the ceiling of the Terrace of Saturn, painted by Giovanni Stradano and not finished until 1562 and 1566. Vasari's main collaborators were Cristofano Gherardi called Doceno (1508-1556) and Marco Marchetti da Faenza, responsible for the majority of the grotesque decorations. The only surviving white and red terracotta tile floor, the one in the Room of Opi, is the work of Santi di Michele Buglioni. In the Room of the Elements we can still admire the original marble fireplace, designed, like the one in the Room of Leo X below, by Bartolomeo Ammannati. The only surviving stained-glass window is the one in the Calliope Study, next to the Room of Ceres: it was made by Walter of Antwerp (second half of the 16th century) on cartoons by Vasari and Marco da Faenza.
In the learned iconographical programme drawn up by Cosimo Bartoli, the dedication of the rooms of this Apartment to the Heavenly Gods was intended to establish a permanent bond with the rooms on the floor below, the Apartment of Leo X, dedicated to the Earthly Gods of the Medici dynasty.

Room of the Elements

This room is dedicated to the Four Elements which the ancients thought were the foundation of the cosmos: *Air*, *Earth*, *Fire* and *Water*.

Ceiling. Scenes related to *Air*. In the middle, *Saturn Mutilates Heaven*; along the sides, beginning from the octagon above the entrance, from left to right, *Allegory of Truth*, *The Sun Chariot*, *Allegory of Peace*, *Allegory of Day*, *Allegory of Fame*, *The Moon Chariot*, *Allegory of Justice*, *Allegory of Night*.

Side walls. On the wall to the left of the entrance, scenes related to *Earth*. From left to right: above the entrance door, in an oval, *Triptolemus Ploughing*, followed by the main panel, *Earth's First Produce Offered to Saturn*, and a *Sacrifice to Cybele* above the other door; below, *Battle of Sea Gods*.
On the end wall, scenes related to *Fire*: above the door leading to the Room of Opi, *Vulcan Finds Mars and Venus Together*, followed by *Vulcan's Forge* and, above the other door, the one leading to the Room of Jove, *Daedalus Making Achilles's Weapons*; below, the original

G. Vasari and assistants
Room of the Elements

fireplace with *Battles between Sea Gods* on either side. On the next wall, scenes related to *Water*: from the left, above the door leading to a small landing, *Offerings to Venus*, followed by the *Birth of Venus* and, above the door leading to the Terrace of Saturn, *Venus and Adonis*. On the window wall: above, grotesque decorations; between the windows, from left to right, *Mercury* and *Pluto*.

Room of Ceres

This room is dedicated to the goddess of fertility and harvest. At present it is not part of the regular visitor's tour, since the Room of Opi, leading to it, has been closed in order to protect the original floor tiles.

Ceiling. In the centre, *Ceres Searching for her Daughter Proserpine*; at the sides, beginning with the roundel above the entrance from the Room of Opi, from left to right: *Apollo*, *Putti with Garland*, *Juno*, *Triptolemus*, *Jove*, *Putti with Garland*, *Diana*, *Arethusa* and *Electra*.

The frieze shows putti with festoons and panels of grotesque decoration.

The Calliope Study

One enters this room from the Room of Ceres. It is named after the Muse of Poetry, but is actually dedicated to all the Muses; it was one of Duke Cosimo's favourite secret rooms, where

G. Vasari and assistants
Saturn Mutilates Heaven (Ceiling of the Room of the Elements)

G. Vasari and assistants
Earth's First Produce Offered to Saturn (Room of the Elements)

G. Vasari and
assistants
Room of Ceres

G. Vasari and
assistants
Ceres Searching for her Daughter Proserpine (Ceiling of the Room of Ceres)

he kept his collections of precious objects and jewels, miniatures and small bronzes.
Ceiling. Calliope Surrounded by the Attributes of the Muses.
The frieze shows Duke Cosimo's heraldic devices; the original stained-glass windows show *The Three Graces Preparing Venus*, between the *Virtues of Faith and Hope* and grotesque decorations.

Room of Opi

The entrance is from the Room of the Elements; the room is named after the goddess of

Marco da Faenza
Detail of the grotesque decorations and the figure of Diana from the ceiling of the Room of Ceres

Walter of Antwerp, after a drawing by G. Vasari and Marco da Faenza
Stained-glass window (The Calliope Study)

Plenty, the wife of Saturn, god of Agriculture.

Ceiling. In the centre, *The Triumph of the Goddess Opi*; at the sides, beginning from the panel above the entrance from the Room of the Elements, from left to right: *Two Putti Embracing, Summer, Two Putti Embracing, Autumn, Two Putti Embracing, Winter, Two Putti Embracing, Spring.*

Frieze. From left to right, beginning from the entrance, *Allegories of the Months*: *May, June, July, August, September, October, November, December, January, February, March, April.*

The floor still preserves its original red and white terracotta tiles; as in the rooms on the floor below, it repeats symmetrically the divisions of the ceiling. In the middle there is the following inscription: "COSM./MEDIC./DUX/FLORE./LI/MDLVI."

G. Vasari and C. Gherardi
Winter (Ceiling of the Room of Opi)

G. Vasari and C. Gherardi
Spring (Ceiling of the Room of Opi)

G. Vasari and assistants
Room of Opi

Room of Jove

This room can be reached through the Room of the Elements. It is dedicated to the father of the gods of classical antiquity and is situated right above the Room of Cosimo I.

Ceiling. In the centre, *The Childhood of Jove*, looked after by the Nymphs and nursed by the she-goat Amalthea; at the sides, beginning from the entrance from the Room of the Elements, from left to right: *Sacrificial Offering, Allegory of Intelligence, Sacrificial Offering, Allegory of Honour, Sacrificial Offering, Allegory of Glory, Sacrificial Offering, Allegory of Generosity*.

Frieze. Putti with classical and mythological landscapes, alternating with grotesque decorations.

Terrace of Juno

This terrace opens off the Room of Jove. It is dedicated to the wife of the father of the gods, in classical mythology. Originally it was an

△
G. Vasari and assistants
Room of Jove

G. Vasari
The Childhood of Jove (Ceiling of the Room of Jove)

open loggia and its slender pietra serena columns must have offered a splendid view over the buildings that stood on the area now occupied by the palace's second courtyard, and over the rest of the city as well, looking towards the Badia and the Bargello. It was closed in and incorporated into the palace during Ammannati's reconstruction, commissioned by Ferdinand I in 1588. Placed on a modern base resembling the fountain in the first courtyard, we find here the original *Putto with a Dolphin* by Andrea del Verrocchio which stood formerly on a fountain in the Medici villa at Careggi.

Ceiling. In the centre, *Juno on a Chariot Drawn by Peacocks*; to the left, *Allegory of Plenty*, to the right, *Allegory of Power.*

Side walls. To the left, within a lavish stucco frame, *Juno, Jove and Io*; to the left, an architectural niche that originally contained a classical statue of Juno; to the right, in a splendid frame, *Juno, Jove and Callisto.*

G. Vasari and assistants
Terrace of Juno

On the lower band of the wall there is a monochrome painted *Fountain with a Putto*; on either side of it, within oval frames, two female figures.

Room of Hercules

This room opens off a "Ricetto," or corridor, with grotesque decorations, which also leads to the rooms where the works of art recovered by Rodolfo Siviero (see below) are exhibited. The room is dedicated to the god of indomitable and supernatural strength, famous for his twelve labours.

Ceiling. In the centre, *Hercules as a Boy Strangles the Serpents*; at the sides, beginning from the entrance, from left to right, some of the hero's labours: *Hercules and Cerberus, Hercules Steals the Apples of the Hesperides, Hercules Slays Cacus, Hercules Kills Antaeus, Hercules Kills Nessus, Hercules Slays the Cretan Bull, Hercules Kills the Hydra of Lerna, Hercules Slays the Nemean Lion.*

Frieze. Decoration with putti, classical landscapes and globes. One of the surviving tapestries used on solemn occasions is preserved in this room; it depicts *Hercules Defeating the Centaurs at Hyppodamia's Wedding.* It was woven by tapestrymaker Giovanni di Bastiano Sconditi (active from 1555 to about 1568) after a cartoon probably by Marco da Faenza.

The Minerva Study

On the ceiling, *Minerva is Born out of Jove's Brain*, in the presence of Hercules with his club, Apollo with the tripod taken from the oracle, Mercury shown in flight, and to the right, Juno with her usual attribute, the peacock.

Terrace of Saturn

Dedicated to the father of Jove, who ate his own children: only Jove, Juno, Pluto and Neptune managed to escape. From this terrace there is a splendid view: from left to right, the Uffizi, the Oltrarno with the Belvedere Fortress overlooking it, Piazza dei Castellani (formerly Piazza del Grano) and the neighbourhood of Santa Croce.

Andrea del Verrocchio
Putto with a Dolphin
(Terrace of Juno)

Marco da Faenza
Hercules Kills the Hydra of Lerna (Room of Hercules)

G. Vasari and assistants
Ceiling of the Room of Hercules

Ceiling. In the centre, *Saturn Devours his Children*; at the sides, beginning from the entrance from the Room of the Elements, from left to right around the central roundel: *Infancy*, *Old Age*, *Youth* and *Maturity*; in the two larger panels, *Saturn Arrives in Latium* and *Saturn and Janus Build Saturnia*.
Along the outer edge of the ceiling there are allegorical representantions of the *Twelve Hours of the Day*; in the four corners, *Fire*, *Air*, *Water* and *Earth*.

In one corner of the terrace, a small bronze *standardholder* in the shape of a monster, by Giambologna, originally from Palazzo Vecchietti in the street of the same name.

Battista del Tasso, G. Vasari and G. Stradano
Terrace of Saturn

THE WORKS OF ART RECOVERED BY RODOLFO SIVIERO

If we now retrace our steps, back to the "Ricetto" or corridor with the grotesque decorations between the Terrace of Juno and the Room of Hercules, we will find a door leading to a series of rooms containing the works of art recovered by the Minister Plenipotentiary Rodolfo Siviero: most of these works of art had been taken away by the Germans during World War II and were not recovered until the end of the war. A few of these extraordinary objects have been lent to other museums in Italy, but at present (1988) many important works are still on exhibit here, such as several classical sarcophagi; there is also a charming *Madonna of Humility* attributed to Masolino da Panicale (1383-1440/47) and a *Madonna and Child* by Rossello di Jacopo Franchi (c1377-1458).

A painting that is of fundamental importance in the study of the history of art is the little *Madonna and Child*, almost unanimously attributed by critics to Masaccio (1401-1428); at the back of this painting there is the coat-of-arms of Cardinal Antonio Casini, elected Cardinal on 24 May 1426. Other important pieces of the collection are a *Pygmalion and Galathea* by Agnolo Bronzino and the cover of a portrait of Francesco Guardi dressed as a soldier painted by Pontormo in 1529-30. The collection also includes several paintings by Venetian 16th-century artists, such as *Venus and Mercury Present their Son Anteros to Jove* by Veronese (1528-1588); two works, *The Slaughter of the First-born in Egypt* and a *Resurrection* by Jacopo Negretti called Palma the Younger (1544-1628); *Leda and the Swan* by Tintoretto (1519-1594); a copy of Leonardo's lost *Leda*, considered to be the most faithful and attributed to Francesco Melzi (1493-1570); and a *Judith and Holofernes* by Peter Paul Rubens (1577-1640), a splendid painting dating from around 1625.

APARTMENT OF ELEANOR

Retracing our steps once again, back through the Apartment of the Elements, we reach a gallery overlooking the Salone dei Cinquecento; this leads us to the Apartment of Eleanor, a group of rooms inhabited in the 16th century by Cosimo I's Spanish wife and her retinue.

The Green Room

The first room we enter is the *Green Room*, which gets its name from the landscape scenes painted on the walls by Ridolfo del Ghirlandaio (1483-1561) between 1540 and 1542, shortly after the ducal family moved to Palazzo Vecchio from the Medici Palace. Unfortunately, the frescoes have been entirely destroyed.

Ceiling. Grotesque decorations with the Medici-Toledo coat-of-arms in the middle, quartered with the ducal coronet and the Habsburg imperial eagle.

The Private Study of Eleanor

Opening off the room, to the left, the tiny *Private Study of Eleanor of Toledo*, with its charming grotesque decoration on the ceiling painted after 1545 by Francesco Salviati.

Ridolfo del Ghirlandaio
The Green Room

Agnolo Bronzino
Eleanor's Chapel

△
Agnolo Bronzino
Deposition, *Annunciation*, *Prophets and Sibyls* (endwall of Eleanor's Chapel)

Agnolo Bronzino and assistants
Moses Strikes the Rock and Brings Forth Water and *Manna Falling from Heaven* (lefthand wall of Eleanor's Chapel)

Agnolo Bronzino
The Crossing of the Red Sea (righthand wall of Eleanor's Chapel)

△
Agnolo Bronzino
The Worship of the Brazen Serpent (entrance wall of Eleanor's Chapel)

Agnolo Bronzino
Ceiling of Eleanor's
Chapel

Eleanor's Chapel

To the right, through a marble door designed by Bartolomeo Ammannati, one enters *Eleanor's Chapel*, frescoed in several stages between 1540 and 1564 by Agnolo Bronzino.

Ceiling. In the centre, the "vultus trifrons," the symbol of the Trinity, painted over the Medici-Toledo coat-of-arms (which is now visible once again, since the paint has faded); at the sides, beginning from the section above the entrance, *St Jerome in Penance*, followed, from left to right, by *St John the Evangelist on the Island of Patmos*, *The Archangel Michael Defeats the Devil* and *St Francis Receives the Stigmata*. In the side corbels, from left to right, *Temperance*, *Justice*, *Fortitude* and *Prudence*.

Side walls. On the entrance wall, *The Worship of the Brazen Serpent*; on the wall to the left, *Moses Strikes the Rock and Brings forth Water*, two small *Angels* with a chalice and orb (attributed to Alessandro Allori, pupil and follower of Bronzino), *Manna Falling from Heaven*. On the wall opposite: in the centre, panel painting showing the *Deposition* (this a second version of the painting, for the original was presented by Duke Cosimo to Granvelle, Charles V's Chancellor, and is now in the Musée des Beaux-Arts at Besançon); on either side, the *Angel of the Annunciation* and the *Madonna*, which replaced an earlier *St John the Baptist* (Lima, Neuhaus) and a *St Cosimo*, now lost.
Above, the *Prophet David* and the *Erytrean Sibyl*. On the next wall, the *Crossing of the Red Sea*.

Room of the Sabine Women

Continuing along the corridor, we pass on our left the entrance to the bridgeway over Via della Ninna leading to the Uffizi Gallery; we then come to a group of rooms in which the Priors and the Gonfalonier lived at the time of the Republic. These were redesigned and decorated by Giorgio Vasari for Duchess Eleanor, between 1561 and 1562. Each one of these rooms is dedicated to a famous woman from antiquity; the Duchess, however, never came to live here, for she died of malaria in Pisa in 1562. The first room is called the *Room of the Sabine Women* from the painting in the centre of the lavishly carved and gilded ceiling; the painting, like the other ones in this room, is the work of Battista Botticelli (second half of the 16th century) who was helped by Giovanni Stradano. The two artists are responsible for

G. Vasari and G. Stradano
Room of the Sabine Women

G. Vasari and G. Stradano
The Sabine Women Make Peace between the Romans and the Sabines (Ceiling of the Room of the Sabine Women)

most of the paintings in the other rooms of this Apartment as well.

Ceiling. In the oval in the centre, *The Sabine Women Make Peace between their Roman Husbands and their Sabine Relatives*; around this, four allegories of *Victories*; at the sides, beginning from the entrance to the Green Room, from left to right: *Peace Sets Fire to Arms*, a *heraldic device* of Cosimo I, *Diana*, *Juno*, a *device*, *Mars*, *Fame*, a *device*, *Concord*, *Fortitude*, a *device*, *Charity*.

Room of Esther

Dedicated to the young Hebrew girl whose story is told in the Bible, and who was granted royal honours because of her virtue.

Ceiling. In the centre, *Ahasuerus Crowns Esther*; at the sides, beginning from the entrance, from left to right, *Medici coats-of-arms and heraldic devices of Cosimo I* alternating with *bird decorations*.

Frieze. From left to right, beginning from the entrance wall, *inscription* with putti dedicated to Eleanor of Toledo, Duchess of Florence and Siena; at the sides, monochrome grisaille ovals against gold backgrounds showing *Haman Ordering that the Jews be Slaughtered* (?), *A Royal Edict in Favour of the Jews is Passed and the Feast of Purim is Instituted*, *Ahasuerus's Banquet*, *Queen Vasti Refuses to Appear before the King*, *Esther's Banquet*, *Haman and Mordecai*, *Esther Appears before Ahasuerus*, *King Ahasuerus Crowns Esther*.
On the wall to the right of the entrance, a marble basin decorated with the Florentine fleur-de-lys (15th century), not originally in this palace.

Room of Penelope

Dedicated to the faithful wife of Ulysses, Homer's mythical hero.

Ceiling. In the centre, *Penelope at her Loom with her Handmaids*; at the sides, beginning from the entrance from the Room of Esther, from left to right, four *River Gods and Goddesses* and two Medici-Toledo *coats-of-arms*, carved, painted and gilded.

Frieze. From the entrance, from left to right: *Ulysses Frees his Companions from Circe's Spell*, *Allegory of Temperance*, *Ulysses Meets Nausicaa on the Island of the Phaeacians*; on the next wall, *Troy Burning*, *Allegory of Prudence*, *Aeolus's Bag*; on the wall opposite the entrance, *Ulysses Blinds Polyphemus*, *Allegory of Charity*, *The Old Nurse Euriclea Recognizes Ulysses*; on the last wall, *Ulysses Returns to Ithaca*, *Allegory*

G. Vasari and
G. Stradano
Room of Esther

of Fortitude, Mercury Orders the Nymph Calypso to Allow Ulysses to Leave.

The pietra serena *fireplace* was carved in the early 20th century (1921) in a Renaissance revival style; its architrave shows a scroll with Giuliano de' Medici's motto "Glovis."

Room of Gualdrada

This room is dedicated to the aristocratic Florentine maiden who, according to legend, would not allow Emperor Otto IV to kiss her, for she would only be kissed by her husband.

Ceiling. In the centre, in an octagonal frame, *Gualdrada Refuses to Kiss Emperor Otto IV*; at the sides, *Dancing putti with flowers and heraldic devices of Cosimo I.*

Frieze. Views of the most beautiful parts of the city, on the occasion of games and celebrations; from left to right, beginning from the entrance from the Room of Penelope, *Festa degli Omaggi in Piazza della Signoria*, *Allegory of Hope*, *A Joust in Piazza Santa Croce*, *View of Ponte Santa Trinita*, *Allegory of Patience*, *View*

G. Vasari and G. Stradano
Esther and Ahasuerus (Ceiling of the Room of Esther)

G. Vasari and G. Stradano
Penelope at her Loom with her Handmaids
(Ceiling of the Room of Penelope)

G. Vasari and G. Stradano
Room of Penelope

▽
G. Stradano
Ulysses Frees his Companions from Circe's Spell (Frieze in the Room of Penelope)

G. Vasari and G. Stradano
The ceiling of the Room of Gualdrada

G. Vasari and G. Stradano
Gualdrada Refuses to Kiss Emperor Otto IV (Ceiling of the Room of Gualdrada)

G. Stradano
Festa degli Omaggi in Piazza della Signoria (Frieze in the Room of Gualdrada)

G. Stradano
A Joust in Piazza Santa Croce (Frieze in the Room of Gualdrada)

of the Old Market Square, *The Giostra del Saracino Tournament in Via Larga* (today's Via Cavour), *Allegory of Faith*, *A Procession in Piazza del Duomo*, *A Popular Celebration in Piazza Santo Spirito*, *Allegory of Justice*, *A Ball Game in Piazza Santa Maria Novella*.

◁
G. Stradano
Ponte Santa Trinita
(Frieze in the Room of Gualdrada)

G. Stradano
Old Market Square
(Frieze in the Room of Gualdrada)

G. Stradano
The Giostra del Saracino Tournament in Via Larga
(Frieze in the Room of Gualdrada)

G. Stradano
A Procession in Piazza del Duomo
(Frieze in the Room of Gualdrada)

G. Stradano
A Popular Celebration in Piazza Santo Spirito (Frieze in the Room of Gualdrada)

G. Stradano
A Ball Game in Piazza Santa Maria Novella (Frieze in the Room of Gualdrada)

CHAPEL OF THE PRIORS

Our visit then continues down a narrow corridor around the structure of the tower, its walls and ceiling decorated with colourful motifs dating from the 14th and 15th centuries. Next we come to the *Chapel of the Priors*, built between 1511 and 1514 by Baccio d'Agnolo (1462-1543) and decorated by Ridolfo del Ghirlandaio for Lorenzo di Piero de' Medici (1492-1519).

Ceiling. In the centre, *The Holy Trinity with Angels and Cherubim*; in the cross-shaped panels around it, from left to right, *St Matthew*, *St John*, *St Mark* and *St Luke*; in the other panels, *Angels Bearing the Symbols of the Passion* and *Angels with Quotations from the Old Testament*.

Side walls. Monochrome gilded *candelabra*

Baccio d'Agnolo and Ridolfo del Ghirlandaio
The Chapel of the Priors

Ridolfo del Ghirlandaio
Annunciation (Chapel of the Priors)

decorations, with inscriptions taken from the Old and New Testaments; on the wall behind the altar, *Madonna and Child with Saints Elizabeth and John the Baptist*, by Fra Mariano da Pescia (second half of the 16th century). On the wall opposite, *Annunciation*, showing the church of Santissima Annunziata as it was before the 17th-century portico was added at the front. Below, *St John the Baptist*, the patron saint of the city of Florence.

SALA DELL'UDIENZA

From the Chapel we reach the *Audience Chamber*, on of the two rooms created in 1470 by Benedetto da Maiano (1442-1497), who simply built a partition wall across a larger room. Construction work also included a carved and gilded *ceiling* and the frieze, designed and executed by Giuliano da Maiano (1432-1490), Francesco Monciatti and Giovanni da Gaiole (second half of the 15th century) between 1470 and 1476 (?). The *marble door* with its *Statue of Justice*, by Benedetto and Giuliano da Maiano, also dates from this same period. The wooden door panels, with portrayals of *Dante* and *Petrarch*, are the work of Giuliano da Maiano and Francesco di Giovanni called Francione (1428-1495). The marble doorway leading into the chapel is the work of Baccio d'Agnolo (1462-1543), while the monogramme of Christ and the inscription above it were added in 1529, at the time of the second Republic. Between 1543 and 1545 Francesco Salviati frescoed the side walls with *Stories from the Life of Furius Camillus*, as well as allegorical and mythological scenes.

Ceiling. Carved, painted and gilded coffered ceiling, with the coat-of-arms of the Florentine people.

Benedetto da Maiano, Francesco Salviati and assistants: Sala dell'Udienza

Benedetto da Maiano
and assistants
Ceiling of the Sala
dell'Udienza

Benedetto da Maiano
and assistants
Detail of the ceiling
of the Sala
dell'Udienza

Frieze. Decorated with lion heads (the celebrated Marzocco, the symbol of the city of Florence) and classical type festoons.

Side walls. To the left, beginning from the entrance to the Chapel, above which we find the *Sacrifice of Isaac* and the Virtues of *Charity*, *Fortitude*, *Hope* and *Faith*, in the middle of the righthand wall, *Camillus Punishes the Traitor from Falerii*; below it, *female allegorical figure* (Generosity ?); on the wall above the windows, within two ovals and a square frame, *Camillus Listens to the Pleas of the Sutrines*, *Allegory of the River Arno, of Florence and of the House of Medici*, and a *Scene from Ancient History*; below, between the windows, *Allegory of Time as Opportunity (Kairos)*, *Mars Defeats a Gaul*, *Diana*, *Allegory of Time with the Attributes of Prudence and Temperance*. Below still, within oval frames, *Adoration of the Sphinx and allegorical representation of the Arno*. On the wall opposite the entrance, above, within oval frames, *Camillus Consecrates a Temple* and *Camillus as an Old Man is Nominated Dictator* (?); between the windows, the mythological figure *Hecate (the Moon)*, *Allegory of Favour*, the mythological figure *Phanes (the Sun)*.
On the wall adjoining the Sala dei Gigli, from left to right: above, at the sides, *Capricorn*, the zodiac sign of Cosimo I; above the door, *Peace Destroys Weapons*; below, at the sides, *Time Seizes Opportunity by the Hair*, *The Triumph of Camillus after the Capture of Veii*, and *Camillus Puts an End to the Weighing of Gold Organized by the Gauls and the Romans, Putting the Romans to Shame*.

Francesco Salviati
The Triumph of Furius Camillus (Sala dell'Udienza)

SALA DEI GIGLI

Through a 15th-century doorway we enter the *Sala dei Gigli*, or Room of the Fleur-de-lys, which gets its name from the gold "gigli" on a blue ground painted on all four walls. Like the previous room, this one too was created thanks to the partitioning of the Sala Grande in the 1470s. The carved and gilded *ceiling* dates from about 1472-76, like the ceiling in the Audience Chamber (Udienza), and is also the work of Giuliano da Maiano and assistants. The *fresco decoration* on the wall opposite the entrance is slightly later (1482-85) and is the work of Domenico Bigordi called Ghirlandaio (1449-1494) and assistants. The *marble doorway* with its rounded tympanum, which has destroyed the righthand section of the central part of the fresco, was opened in 1589 in order to reach the Room of the Maps.

Ceiling. Carved, painted in blue and gilded, coffered, with gold fleur-de-lys on a blue ground.

Frieze. Carved, painted and gilded with Marzocco lions holding the arms of the Commune, the People and the Guelph Party of Florence.

Side walls. On the wall opposite the entrance, from left to right, above the windows: *Brutus*, *Mutius Scaevola* and *Furius Camillus*, *Decius Mure*, *Scipio Africanus* and *Cicero*; in the centre, *St Zenobius between Saints Stephen and Lawrence*, between two *Marzocco lions bearing*

Benedetto da Maiano, Giuliano da Maiano and Francione
Doorway between the Sala dell'Udienza and the Sala dei Gigli

Benedetto da Maiano and assistants
Domenico Ghirlandaio and assistants
Sala dei Gigli

Domenico Ghirlandaio and assistants
St Zenobius between Saints Stephen and Lawrence (Sala dei Gigli)

Domenico Ghirlandaio and assistants *Brutus, Mutius Scaevola and Furius Camillus* (Sala dei Gigli)

▽
Donatello
Judith and Holofernes
(Sala dei Gigli)

the arms of the People and the City of Florence. Above the door leading to the Audience Chamber, a marble sculpture of the *Young St John* by Benedetto da Maiano, placed between two pairs of *putti with candlesticks*. The statue of *Judith* by Donatello (1386-1466), restored by the Opificio delle Pietre Dure in Florence between 1987 and 1988, is now exhibited in this room; it stood originally in the garden of the Medici Palace in Via Larga and after 1495 it was moved to Piazza della Signoria, where it remained until it was restored. Scholars believe that Donatello carved it around 1453 for the Opera del Duomo in Siena, but it was then bought by the Medici for their palace (cf. Antonio Natali).

THE CHANCERY

Through what was originally a 14th-century window, on the lefthand side of the wall opposite the entrance, there is a small room which was probably the Chancery in the late 15th and early 16th centuries: it was probably in this room that *Niccolò Machiavelli* (1469-1527) worked in his capacity as Cancelliere Dettatore at the time of the Republic (1494-1512). The room contains a *stucco bust* (16th century) of Machiavelli and a posthumous *portrait* by Santi di Tito. On the end wall there is a bas-relief of *St George and the Dragon* which stood originally on the gate of San Giorgio on the city walls.

Donatello
Detail of the head of *Judith*

SALA DELLE CARTE GEOGRAFICHE

Returning into the *Sala dei Gigli*, through a doorway with a marble tympanum we enter the *Sala delle Carte Geografiche*, Room of the Maps, designed between 1563 and 1565 by Giorgio Vasari. The *wood cupboards* were carved by Dionigi di Matteo Nigetti, while the *Maps* were painted by Fra Egnazio Danti (1536-1586) and Fra Stefano Bonsignori (?-1589) before 1581.

In the centre of the room there is a large *globe* made by Danti between 1564 and 1568.

G. Vasari, D. Nigetti, E. Danti and S. Bonsignori
Sala delle Carte Geografiche

E. Danti
Italy (Sala delle Carte Geografiche)

E. Danti
France (Sala delle
Carte Geografiche)

E. Danti
Germany (Sala delle
Carte Geografiche)

E. Danti
England (Sala delle Carte Geografiche)

SALOTTA

After the *Room of the Maps* and the *Sala dei Gigli*, on the other side of the landing at the top of the stairway, we come to the *Salotta*, where two detached frescoes show what Palazzo Vecchio looked like in the 14th and 15th centuries: the first fresco, originally in the former prison of the Stinche, depicts *The Expulsion of the Tyrant Walter de Brienne, Duke of Athens,* which took place on 26 July 1343, on the feast day of St Anne (who is shown seated on a throne in the act of blessing the Florentine standards); the other, from the Girolami Tower in Por Santa Maria, depicts *St Zenobius* with Piazza della Signoria in the background.

Unknown 15th-century artist
St Zenobius (Salotta)

A. Orcagna
The Expulsion of the Duke of Athens
(Salotta)

SALA DELLE BANDIERE

Returning to the landing outside the *Salotta*, to the left a steep stairway leads us to the gallery around the palace and the tower; also on this floor is the *Sala delle Bandiere*, or Room of the Flags, a huge room built in 1886 in order to house the flags that the Municipalities of Italy had donated to Florence in 1865. At present this room contains a technical laboratory working on the restoration of the famous tapestry series of *Stories of Joseph* from the Old Testament, woven in the Medici tapestry factory between 1546 and 1553 on cartoons by Pontormo, Bronzino and Salviati. The restoration is financed by the City of Florence and by the Cassa di Risparmi e Depositi of Prato; the highly specialized staff involved in this work is supervised by the restorers and directors of the Opificio delle Pietre Dure.

The stairway leading to the tower

The Sala delle Bandiere, with the technical laboratory working on the restoration of the tapestries from the Sala dei Dugento.

The Rope Room

Mezzanine Floor

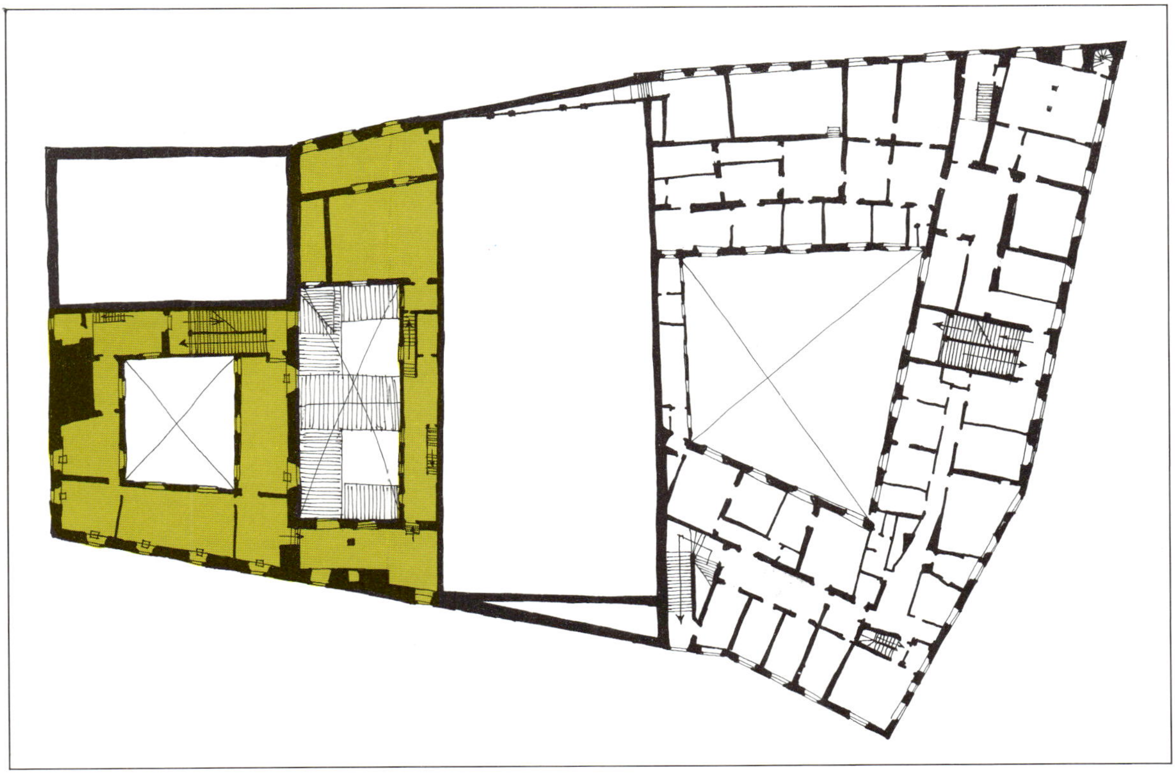

Ground-plan of the Mezzanine Floor
These rooms contain the collection of musical instruments and the Loeser Bequest

To reach the floor below we go down the so-called *Scala Piana*, or Flat Stairway, built by Vasari in 1561; it takes us to the *Mezzanine floor*, created by Michelozzo when he lowered the ceilings of the first floor rooms as part of his general redesigning of the palace around 1453.
In the first rooms we come to we find a collection of antique *musical instruments*, belonging to the Luigi Cherubini Musical Conservatoires in Florence; they are only on temporary exhibit here, until a more suitable location is found.
The other rooms contain the works of the Loeser Bequest, now the property of the City of Florence; this collection includes a *Madonna and Child* by the Sienese artist Pietro Lorenzetti (c1280-1348?), a painted *Cross* by an unknown Sienese artist dating from about 1280, a *Madonna and Child* by the Master of the Griggs Crucifixion (Giovanni Toscani?, d. 1420), a lovely embroidery of the *Dead Christ* and the *Mater Dolorosa* made on a design by Raffaellino del Garbo (1466-1525), two terracotta groups of *Battles between Knights* by Giovan Francesco Rustici (1474-1554), a roundel of the *Madonna and Child with the Young St John* by the Spanish painter Alonso Berruguete (c1486-1561), the splendid portrait of the *Poetess Laura Battiferri*, the wife of the sculptor and architect Bartolomeo Ammannati, by Agnolo Bronzino and a small fresco on a brick tile of a *Battle between Knights*, a preparatory sketch for the Capture of the Tower of San Vincenzo in the Salone dei Cinquecento painted by Giovan Battista Naldini.

G. Vasari
The "Flat Stairway"

Michelozzo
Room of the Golden Fleur-de-lys

△
Michelozzo
A room on the Mezzanine Floor

Bronzino
Portrait of Laura Battiferri (Mezzanine)

RICETTO

At the foot of the stairway we come to the "Ricetto." The ceiling here was frescoed by Lorenzo Sabatini (c1530-1576) with allegorical figures, as well as Medici and Imperial emblems and coats-of-arms.

Ceiling. Above the door to the left of the stairway, which leads to the Sala dei Dugento, there are two allegorical female figures personifying *Concord* and *Mercurial Virtue*, that is the love of the powerful for letters and the arts; next, in an octagonal frame, *Allegory of Prudence*, followed by an oval with *putti* playing with the Medici coat-of-arms, the ducal coronet and the emblem of the Golden Fleece, an honour Cosimo I was awarded in 1544. In the following section of the ceiling, *Allegory of Justice*, and in the lunette above the door leading to the Salone dei Cinquecento, *Allegory of Peace* and of *Victory*; below, a *bust of Cosimo I de' Medici* by the school of Baccio Bandinelli.

SALA DEI DUGENTO

From the *Ricetto* we enter the *Sala dei Dugento*, normally closed to the public because it is here that the meetings of the Town Council are held.
This room was part of the original 14th-century structure of the palace and has always been used as a Council Room; the ceiling and the carved friezes date from 1472 and are the work of Benedetto da Maiano and his brother Giuliano, helped by assistants. The two *marble doorways* with triangular tympanums date from the early 16th century and are the work of Baccio d'Agnolo.

The coffered *ceiling* is decorated with fleur-de-lys and rosettes; the frieze is ornamented with festoons containing the arms of the Florentine Republic.

The series of *tapestries of Stories from the Life of Joseph* from the Old Testament, currently being restored in the laboratory in the Sala delle Bandiere, originally hung in this room.

Benedetto da Maiano and assistants
Sala dei Dugento

SALA DEGLI OTTO

There is another small room that opens off the Ricetto, the *Sala degli Otto*, also used by the Town Council administration; it has a carved *ceiling* decorated with cherub heads and fleur-de-lys dating from the same period as the ceiling decorations in the Sala dei Dugento and in the Audience Chamber and Sala dei Gigli on the floor above. A mosaic *Madonna and Child* dating from the 14th century is kept in this room, and on the walls there are two round *coats-of-arms* dating from the second half of the 16th century (in the 18th century the Medici arms were replaced by the Lorraine arms).

APARTMENT OF COSIMO I

Before leaving Palazzo Vecchio, just a few words about the *Apartment* in which Cosimo I de' Medici lived. It is on the first floor, opposite the main entrance to the Salone dei Cinquecento, on the other side of the landing at the top of Vasari's grand Stairway. At present it houses administrative offices. Today there are not many signs of the former grandeur and importance of these apartments: a small *bathroom* with grotesque decorations by Marco

G. Vasari and Marco da Faenza Cosimo I's Bathroom

da Faenza and two *allegorical figures* in the intrados above the window in what was probably the *bedroom of Cosimo I*, a room adjoining Francesco I's Studiolo.

In this small room the ceiling originally had frescoes by Vasari, painted between 1559 and 1561, depicting *Solomon Asleep*, *Famous Men of Antiquity* and *Allegorical Figures*. These frescoes were destroyed by architect Carlo Falconieri in 1865 when he restructured the rooms of the palace so as to make it suitable for the Chamber of Deputies during the period when Florence was the capital of Italy. Falconieri also designed a new stairway alongside the existing spiral one which connects Cosimo's bedroom to the street below, Via della Ninna. Tradition has it that the spiral staircase was built at the time of the Duke of Athens

G. Vasari and assistants
The "Tesoretto"

The stairway leading to the tower

The "Alberghettino", where Cosimo the Elder was imprisoned in 1433 and Fra Girolamo Savonarola in 1498

(1342-43). From the Studiolo, down a stairway built into the walls of the palace, we come to the "*Tesoretto*," the private study where the Duke kept his jewels and his precious possessions; this room is so small that for security reasons it cannot be opened to the public.

Coat-of-arms of Ludovico di Tommaso di Ronco Sighifredo from Reggio, the Captain of the People who arrested and imprisoned Cosimo the Elder in the "Alberghettino" in 1433

Short Bibliography

C. CONTI, *La prima reggia di Cosimo I de' Medici*, Firenze, 1893.

A. LENSI, *Palazzo Vecchio*, Milano-Roma, 1929.

J. WILDE, *The Hall of the Great Council of Florence*, in "Journal of the Warburg and Courtauld Institutes", VII, 1944, pp. 65-81.

U. BALDINI, *Palazzo Vecchio ẹ i quartieri monumentali*, Firenze, 1950.

G. SINIBALDI, *Il Palazzo Vecchio di Firenze*, Roma, 1969.

E. ALLEGRI-A. CECCHI, *Palazzo Vecchio e i Medici, guida storica*, Firenze, 1980.

Index of artists

The index refers to the artists mentioned in the text. Numbers in bold face refer to illustrations